W9-BMO-744

MELANNIE SVOBODA, SND

By the Way

100

REFLECTIONS
ON THE
SPIRITUAL LIFE

By the Way

100 REFLECTIONS
ON THE SPIRITUAL LIFE

By the Way

100 REFLECTIONS
ON THE SPIRITUAL LIFE

MELANNIE SVOBODA, SND

TWENTY
THIRD 23rd
PUBLICATIONS

DEDICATION

To these wonderful Sisters of Notre Dame:

Dion, Ellenann, Lenette, Mary Fran, Patti, and Shauna

Thank you for walking "The Way" with me

Twenty-Third Publications
A Division of Bayard
One Montauk Avenue, Suite 200
New London, CT 06320
(860) 437-3012 or (800) 321-0411
www.23rdpublications.com

ISBN 978-1-58595-830-6
Library of Congress Control Number: 2011923255
Printed in the U.S.A.

CONTENTS

Introduction   1

SUMMER

1. The Unfairness of Love and Mercy   4
2. Heroic Honesty   5
3. A Prophet Next Door   6
4. On Any Given Day   7
5. Approachable Jesus   8
6. Where God Lives   9
7. Sleep   10
8. The Times We Live In   11
9. Coming in for a Landing   12
10. Meerkats Soaking up the Sun   13
11. "Your Love Holds Me Up"   14
12. St. Paul's Chapel in New York City   15
13. God's Best Shot   16
14. Consider This   17
15. Sing!   18
16. The Humor of Children   19
17. Writing Begets Writing   20
18. Friendship with Jesus   20
19. Quotations on Leadership   21
20. Haunted by God   22

21. Holy Doubt   23

22. The Mystery of the Shrinking Teddy Bear   24

23. Something Is Asked of Me   25

24. "All Summer in a Day"   26

25. Why Is There So Much Goodness?   27

FALL

26. Earth Tilts   30

27. Our Hope Lies in _____   31

28. Meditation on an Apple   32

29. Saints and Work   34

30. The Individual and the Community   35

31. Walking   36

32. The Birth of a Panda   38

33. September 8: Mary's Birthday   39

34. As Others See Us   40

35. Jesus Is a Thief in the Night   41

36. "Poet and Peasant Overture"   42

37. Freed from Prison   43

38. I Am Not Alone   43

39. Where Do We Aim Our Cameras?   45

40. The Burning Bush   46

41. Whom Do Atheists Thank?   47

42. The Parking Space   48

43. The Wonder of Healing   49

44. Quotations about God   50

45. The Bird Guard   51

46. Finding Humor Everywhere   52

47. I Want to Go Back, God   53

48. The Flying Trapeze Artist   54

49. Waiting and Watching   55

50. A Tap on the Shoulder   56

WINTER

51. The Lesson of the Afghan   60

52. The Christmas Mug   61

53. Survival   62

54. Old Aunts and Old Houses   63

55. The Concordance to the Bible   64

56. Dispossession   65

57. St. Paul   66

58. Compassion   67

59. Inklings   68

60. Poor Me   69

61. "I Am with You Always"   70

62. Dressing Room Mirrors   70

63. The Miracle of Being   72

64. The Christmas "Giving Tree"   72

65. The God of Many Chances   73

66. We Are Sojourners   74

67. I Don't Want to Live
     in This World Any Longer   75
68. St. Joseph   76
69. Let Real Life Begin—Again   77
70. Quotations on Adversity   78
71. On Beauty and Becoming Human   79
72. Winter: The Misunderstood Season   80
73. Jigsaw Puzzles   81
74. Heroes of Social Justice   82
75. At Home with Death   83

SPRING

76. Quotations on Spring   88
77. Did Jesus Dance?   89
78. My To-Do List   90
79. Wondering about Death
     at a Baseball Game   91
80. God's Voice Mail   92
81. God Wants Me to Be _____   92
82. The Annunciation   93
83. More Inklings   94
84. Blessed Un-assurance   95
85. Necessary Burdens   95
86. Notice What You Notice   96
87. The Book of Jonah   97
88. The Need for Security   99

89. Six Reasons to Be Hopeful   99

90. God's Greatest Stoop   101

91. The 300-Year-Old Oak Tree   102

92. Quotations on Love   103

93. Plan B   104

94. Easter   105

95. Beginning Anew   107

96. Two Mothers-in-Law in Scripture   108

97. Humor Can Save Us   109

98. The Lessons of Life   111

99. Small, Imperfect Stones   112

100. Freedom: Doing What I Ought   113

Index   115

INTRODUCTION

By the way. It's a phrase we hear and say all the time: "By the way, your mother called...By the way, would you stop for some milk on your way home today?" The phrase usually precedes something we almost forgot to say. Or it means there's something important we want to say, but it doesn't quite fit into the current conversation: "By the way, the car is making a funny noise."

This book is called *By the Way* for several reasons. First, it is a collection of things I've wanted to say but which didn't fit into the "conversation" of my previous books. This book is saying, "By the way, here are a hundred more things I'd like to say."

I also chose the title because the word "way" is found frequently in Scripture. In the Psalms, we read things like this: "Teach me your *way*, Lord" (27:11), "[God] teaches the humble the *way*" (25:9), and "Wait eagerly for the Lord, and keep to the *way*" (37:34). The word "way" in these instances suggests a manner of living that is in accord with God's direction and designs.

There's more. In the early church, the phrase "The Way" was synonymous with Christianity itself. In Acts, we read that St. Paul, before his dramatic conversion, persecuted "anyone who belonged to *The Way*" (Acts 9:2), that is, anyone who was a follower of Jesus. And Jesus himself said those memorable words, "I am *the way*, the truth and the life" (John 14:6). This book is intended especially for people striving to live their lives *by The Way*.

The short reflections in this book cover a variety of topics: faith, family, friendship, nature, joy, pain, humor, prayer, and so forth. They arose, for the most part, while I was engaged in the ordinary tasks of daily living: cooking supper, walking in the park, praying with Scripture, reading the newspaper, playing with children, riding in a golf cart, eating an apple, surfing the Net, giving a talk, watching a TV program on ostriches. They are grouped under the four seasons of the year. Though reflections for Christmas can be found under winter and those about Easter under spring, most of the reflections are appropriate for any time of year. Each reflection concludes with a brief prayer. At the end of the book is an index to help you locate particular topics that were mentioned.

It is my hope that *By the Way* will help and encourage you to follow The Way shown to us by Jesus himself. (By the way, you can let me know what you think of this book or share with me some of your own "by the way reflections" by writing to me at The Sisters of Notre Dame, 13000 Auburn Road, Chardon, OH 44024.)

SUMMER

"In summer, the song sings itself."

WILLIAM CARLOS WILLIAMS

1. *The Unfairness of Love and Mercy*

Most of us are born with a keen sense of justice. Even as small children, we knew when something was not fair. If our brother got the bigger cookie, if our sister was allowed to stay up later than we were, or if it wasn't our turn to feed the dog and yet we were told to feed him, we were quick to protest, "That's not fair!"

No wonder Jesus' teachings on love are so hard for us to accept. They often go against this innate sense of justice. Jesus says, "When someone strikes you on your right cheek, turn the other one to him as well" (Mt 5:39). I find myself protesting: "Heck no! I'm going to slap him back!"

Jesus says, "...from the person who takes your cloak, do not withhold even your tunic" (Lk 6:29). "Are you kidding?" I ask. "Why, I might even steal her shoes!"

Jesus says we are to forgive our brothers and sisters "not seven times, but seventy-seven times" (Mt 18:22). I sometimes say, "Are you serious? You mean if someone wrongs me, hurts me, or treats me like dirt, I'm supposed to say, 'That's okay. I forgive you'? Not me! That's not fair!"

But when we recall God's incredible and everlasting love for us, we realize: That's not fair either. That this God of Goodness, Power, Beauty, and Truth should love (as the old hymn says) "a wretch like me" is the epitome of unfairness. But our faith assures us it's a fact. God does love us—freely, unconditionally, gratuitously. In fact, both our existence and our salvation are rooted squarely in the unfairness of God's love and mercy for us.

So, like it or not, we who call ourselves Christians are commanded to love others as God loves us: freely and forgivingly. To do otherwise wouldn't be fair.

God of love and mercy, help me to love others as unfairly as you love me!

2. Heroic Honesty

I was having lunch with my eighty-four-year-old mother in a restaurant near where I live. It was a hot June day. Suddenly two young girls walked by our table clad in rather skimpy outfits— short shorts and halter tops. After they had passed, my mother leaned forward and asked softly, "Did you see the way those two girls were dressed?"

"Yes," I replied.

My mother shook her head a few times. After a moment, though, she began to chuckle.

"What's so funny?" I asked.

She replied, "I was just thinking, maybe I'm a little jealous!" And she laughed some more.

When we think of heroism, we think of battlefields, hospital wards, courtrooms, and such. But that day my mother displayed another kind of heroism: honesty with oneself. She traced her own critical attitude down to its roots and found a trace of jealousy there. What great courage that takes.

Maybe we, too, should explore the roots of our negative attitudes. We might be surprised at what we find there: jealousy, loneliness, fear, laziness, pride.

God of truth, keep me honest—especially with myself and with you.

3. A Prophet Next Door

We might enjoy listening to a prophet every now and then, but I don't think we'd like to live next door to one, work on a committee with one, or invite one over for a cookout. Prophets are always stirring up trouble. They never let things just be. They're not known for their tact, either, but are often outspoken. Prophets offend people, too—especially those who have something to lose—like us, like me. The only people they seem to please are those who not only have nothing to lose but who also have nothing. Period.

Many of us consider prophets unrealistic, for prophets actually believe a better world is possible. Many of us, in contrast, have accepted the fact that what we see today is probably as good as it's ever going to get. Prophets never mind their own business either, but are always poking their noses into everybody else's business—including our own. They make it seem as if we are somehow to blame that the world isn't a better place to live in—as if we actually contribute to the evil in the world by the things we do or don't do. Prophets harp on certain themes again and again, like: "Repent...Forgive...Share...Change your ways...People are suffering. What are *you* doing about it?"

It's little wonder we don't invite prophets to our cookouts—or anywhere else. They make us uncomfortable. They make us feel guilty.

God of all true prophecy, attune my ears and heart to what today's prophets are saying—no matter how uncomfortable or guilty it makes me feel.

4. *On Any Given Day*

On any given day, even a lousy baseball team with a record of 10-57 can beat a great team with a record of 62-5. That's what makes baseball so interesting, so exciting. Any team can win a game on any given day.

A case in point: the 1969 New York Mets. In 1962, the Mets' debut season, they were 40-120. The next few years they raised their win-loss record from lousy to mediocre, starting their 1969 season 11-10. But by the end of the season, things had changed. They won 38 of their last 49 games and went on to win the World Series despite their underdog status.

If lousy teams always lost and great teams always won, no one would play or watch the game of baseball.

I wonder if the same thing is true in the spiritual and moral realm.

On any given day, can goodness "win" over evil—even if goodness has a lousy track record? On any given day, can a seemingly mediocre individual perform an extraordinary act of love and courage? I believe so. In fact, I think this is precisely what hope is all about. Hope is the virtue that believes in the triumph of good over evil, the extraordinary over the mediocre—maybe not every time, but perhaps *this* time. And *ultimately* for sure. Hope is a precious gift Jesus bequeathed to us. It's a gift he taught through some unforgettable parables that said things like this: Lost sheep can be found and be returned to the fold; a grain of wheat can produce a hundredfold; renegade sons do return home; and good Samaritans do happen by just in the nick of time.

But Jesus did more than direct us to *hope* that good things will happen. He gave us a pattern for living that actually *makes* good things happen. By following Jesus' way, we make what we hope for a reality.

Today is any given day. May my pattern of Christian living make good things happen.

5. Approachable Jesus

Jesus was extremely approachable. All kinds of people were drawn to him: Jews and Gentiles, men and women, rich and poor, healthy and sick, young and old—even little children. People were drawn not only by his words and teachings but also by his mien and demeanor. There must have been gentleness in his bearing, understanding in his facial expression, and compassion in his gaze for so many people to be attracted to him.

Someone has said that the greatest sin is to make God unattractive. Jesus did the exact opposite. He made God extremely attractive. He showed us God as Abba, Father, Daddy, Mother, Mommy. He convinced us that God is someone who is concerned about us, attentive to us, wants good for us. In short, Jesus taught that God was indeed approachable—just as he himself was!

A good question to ask ourselves is this: How approachable am I? Do I witness to an attractive God?

Approachable Jesus, help me to witness today to an attractive God.

6. Where God Lives

A friend of mine, a widow, owns a golf course in my area. One evening I went for supper at her house, which is nestled among some trees right next to the links. When I got out of my car, she greeted me with, "Come with me. I want to show you where God lives." We hopped onto her golf cart and began to ride all over the course, careful not to get in the way of the golfers who were trying to get a game in before dark.

As we bounced up and down the hills, my friend would periodically stop the cart at a particularly pretty spot and say, "Now, don't you think God lives there?" She would direct my attention to a small grove of pine trees, a glistening lake, a vista of lush green hills. Every time she asked me, "Don't you think God lives there?" I could only say a resounding, "Yes, I do!"

Later that evening, as we prayed together, we came across a line in a book that said we must take time to look for God's presence in our lives. She remarked, "That's exactly what we just did on the golf course today, didn't we?" I agreed.

Of course, God doesn't live only in pretty places. God lives in ordinary or even seemingly ugly places as well. God resides not only on a beautifully landscaped golf course, but under a dirty bridge in an old city, on a noisy assembly line, in a stark prison cell. God lives not only in harmony, clarity, and joy, but also in messiness, confusion, and pain.

But I think we must start by looking for God in the loveliness of life: a stately oak, the smile of a baby, a long-lasting friendship. Once we get used to spotting God in beauty, we will begin to find God in *all* the places of our lives. We will then have a renewed appreciation of that simple Baltimore Catechism question and answer: "Where is God?" "God is everywhere."

God of everywhere, may I find you living in both the beauty and confusion of my present life.

7. *Sleep*

The invention of the light bulb has been a marvelous gift for civilization. At the same time, it has its "dark side." The light bulb has enabled us to turn night into day. We can stay up to work or play twenty-four hours a day if we want to. It is not surprising then that some doctors are now saying that many people in so-called modern civilizations are essentially sleep-deprived.

A lack of sleep disturbs the body. It makes us sluggish, irritable, unable to concentrate. Some believe it even lowers our natural immunity to colds and disease. But a lack of sleep also disturbs the spiritual life. It can make us discouraged, fearful, and overwhelmed with doubts. That's why one key way to sustain or regain a healthy spirituality is simply to get sufficient sleep. During sleep, many blessings are bestowed: We receive strength to face the challenges of daily living, we gain new insights into difficult situations, we receive patience to deal with so-called problem people, and we discover answers to nagging questions.

It is no coincidence that in Scripture, God often communicates to individuals while they are sleeping: Jacob (Gen 32:24–32), Samuel (1 Sam 3:1–18), and St. Joseph (Mt 1:18–25), to name a few.

Loving God, I thank you for the gift of sleep. Please continue to give me counsel even in the night.

8. *The Times We Live In*

Some of the saints lived during terrible times. Take St. Catherine of Siena, who lived in fourteenth-century Italy. During her time, the Black Death raged throughout Europe, mercenary armies prowled the countryside waging war everywhere, and Pope Gregory XI was cowering in Avignon, France, leaving the administration of the Church in the hands of corrupt legates. In many ways, it was the worst of times.

But Catherine did not bemoan her times. She did not say, "If only the Black Death would go away...If only the world were at peace...If only we had perfect Church leaders, then I could really live my Christian faith." No, Catherine became a great saint precisely by accepting her times as the context in which God was calling her to live her faith. She did not run away from the critical issues of her day; rather, she engaged with them.

Sometimes we are quick to bemoan the times in which we live. We assume that the world used to be a kinder and gentler place or that our ancestors had it easier than we do. But a quick perusal of history would dispel such a view. It would show that every age could be called "the worst of times" for one reason or another. For every age has its serious challenges and dire problems—just as our times do. But, as Christians, we believe that our age is the very context in which we are being called to live out our faith. We are being called to respond to the serious problems and issues of our times in the same way St. Catherine responded to hers: with attentiveness, love, courage, ingenuity, persistence, and great faith in Jesus.

> *Jesus, Lord of all times, help me to respond to the challenges of my times with attentiveness,*

*love, courage, ingenuity, persistence, and great
faith in you.*

9. *Coming in for a Landing*

I was sitting on a bench by a small lake one day when I suddenly heard the honking of some geese. I looked up to see a small flock of geese (eleven to be exact) coming in for a landing on the lake. I watched with fascination as they lowered their wings, decreased their speed, stuck out their webbed feet, and glided gently down upon the water with barely a ripple. I wanted to clap and yell to them from the shore, "Bravo! Well done!"

I wonder how long it takes a goose to learn to land—especially on water. I imagine the first few times a goose tries it, he or she may come in too hard and go SPLASH! Or perhaps a goose may even overshoot the pond altogether if the pond is small.

My nephew Matt, a pilot, always says that when it comes to flying an airplane, it is the landing that demands the greatest skill. This is so because the pilot has to take into consideration many variables while landing: wind velocity, wind direction, the length and width of the runway, the condition of the runway, airplane weight, and airplane speed.

Says Matt, "Crosswinds can be especially tricky. Let's say the wind is blowing left to right. To correct for this, the plane wants to turn left, so the pilot hits the rudder to align the nose with the runway. The pilot also has to dip the left wing down so that the wind won't blow the plane to the right. Strong or gusting winds require more effort of the pilot."

That's why every time I'm flying and we come in for a landing and I feel the plane's wheels touch the ground, I want to clap for the pilots up front who make such a difficult maneuver look so easy.

The sight of the geese landing in the lake and my own experience of flying led me to reflect on our final landing, our death. When we die, we're coming in for a landing into eternity, our final "resting place." I hope when I die I can land with grace and confidence. I hope that all the practice I've had in letting go throughout my life will serve me well when, at death, I am asked to let go of virtually *everything*. And when I find myself finally landing safely on the other side of death, I hope I hear God (and my loved ones who have preceded me in death) clapping and saying, "Bravo, Melannie! Well done!"

God of my life, when it's time for me to make my final landing, bless me with courage, grace, and confidence.

10. Meerkats Soaking Up the Sun

Meerkats, members of the mongoose family, are found primarily in southern Africa. Weighing only about one-and-a-half to two pounds, they resemble elongated, scrawny prairie dogs. They have long, thin tails, too, which they use to balance themselves while standing on their hind legs. Meerkats live in communities of about twenty to thirty members. Adept burrowers, they dig intricate networks of underground tunnels for sleeping in, shielding their young pups, and escaping from predators.

Many aspects of meerkat behavior are interesting. For example, they run day care centers. This means a couple of adults stay at home and babysit the community's pups while the others go out in search of food. Meerkats also groom each other regularly. It supposedly facilitates bonding. They love to play, too, but while they frolic, one meerkat, the designated sentry, stands erect scanning the horizon and the sky for danger.

One behavior I find especially intriguing is this: Every morning, meerkats start their day by quietly standing on their hind legs, facing the sun and absorbing its rays. There is a practical reason for this routine, of course. After a night in their burrow, the meerkats are often damp and chilled when they first get out of bed. They rely on the sun to dry them off and warm them up before they go about their meerkat business—which mostly means foraging for insects and avoiding predators.

But I can't help but liken what the meerkats do each morning to what I do each morning. I begin my day with prayer. This means I sit quietly each morning—in chapel or in my bedroom—and I soak up the rays—not of the sun, but of the *son*—God's Son. It is a practice that warms me and gives me energy to go about my human business for the day.

Jesus, Son of God, may I begin each day by soaking up the rays of your love.

11. *"Your Love Holds Me Up"*

When I was sixteen, a group of boys threw me into a lake that was about twenty feet deep. At that time in my life, I didn't know how to swim. Terrified, I splashed around for several seconds, certain I was going to drown. Suddenly, I felt a pair of hands around my waist pushing me up and out of the water, where I gasped for air. One of the boys had jumped in and saved me.

In the Psalms we find these words: "Your love, Lord, holds me up" (94:18). Every time I pray these words I am reminded of that time I nearly drowned. It is easy for me now to imagine God's strong hands around my waist holding my head above the struggles of daily life lest I drown. What struggles? The struggle of relating compassionately to others, trying to make ends meet, experiencing pain, growing old, worrying about the future, trying to do the right thing.

God of my salvation, make me more aware of your love holding me up today. And if I meet people who are drowning or slipping, help me to hold them up in any way I can.

12. St. Paul's Chapel in New York City

A couple of years ago, I had the privilege of visiting St. Paul's Chapel in New York City. This small, old church is situated directly across the street from where the World Trade Center once stood. Following 9/11, this small Christian community opened its doors to recovery workers and clean-up personnel. Twenty-four hours a day for many months, the church community provided free meals, cots to sleep on, medical aid, prayer, counseling services, and even massage therapy for the many weary workers seeking a break from their exhausting labors.

In the first letter of St. John we read: "For whoever is begotten by God conquers the world. And the victory that conquers the world is our faith" (5:4). Yes, our faith does conquer the world—not through brute force or violence, but through gentle compassion and tender love. Our faith prompts us to reach out and help others—sometimes in ways we never imagined we would or could.

> *Jesus, may my faith be expressed today in compassionate acts of love.*

13. *God's Best Shot*

In 1999, I became the leader of my religious community of 440 sisters. When I was first asked to assume this responsibility, I was understandably afraid. I shared some of my fears with a priest friend, adding, "But I'm going to give this new job my best shot!" He was quiet for a moment, and then he said, "Melannie, did you ever stop to think that maybe you are *God's* best shot? That God is actually happy and eager to work through you in this new ministry?"

It's easy for us to believe that God worked through people like St. Teresa of Avila, Abraham Lincoln, Mahatma Gandhi, Dorothy Day, Martin Luther King Jr., Mother Teresa of Calcutta. But can we also believe that God is working *through us*? Do we believe that God is happy and eager to work through us in whatever circumstances we find ourselves today? If we do believe this, then how grateful we should be. And how freed from unnecessary fear and anxiety!

Our Christian faith tells us, God and I are partners. What a duo we make!

> *God, I thank you for allowing me to partner with you to bring about your reign.*

14. *Consider This*

In the gospels, Jesus is always urging his disciples to consider things. "Consider the fig tree," he says. "Consider the lilies of the field, the birds of the air, or this particular parable I am about to share with you." (The etymology of the word "consider" is an interesting one. It literally means "among the stars.")

Jesus seems to be telling his followers (and that includes us!) that we are meant not merely to experience the various aspects of our daily life—the people we interact with, the work we do, the obstacles we meet, the natural world we live in. We are meant to consider these aspects, that is, to take time to reflect upon them, to ponder their meaning and significance. *Why* do we do this? So that we may catch a glimpse of the ways God is active and alive in those daily events and in ourselves. *How* do we do this? By bringing the "stuff" of our daily life to our prayer, by sharing what's happening in our lives with a trusted friend or two, and by trying to apply Scripture to our own circumstances.

The very fact that you are reading a book like this is a good sign that you are probably someone who is already heeding Jesus' words, "Consider this…"

> *Jesus, help me to be a more considering person.*

15. *Sing!*

Here's a question:

Of all the commands God gave to the Israelites throughout the Old Testament, which command was most frequently repeated?
    a) repent   b) believe   c) forgive   d) sing

Take your time. (Hint: Look at the title of this reflection.) What is your final answer? If you said "sing," you're right!

Here's another question: Why was God so intent on having the Israelites sing? Perhaps it was because God knew that singing gets us in touch with our deeper selves, our inmost being, our unfathomable hopes and desires. Who doesn't get a little emotional when "Danny Boy" is sung at an Irish wake? Who can remain sad when a huge chorus begins to sing Beethoven's "Ode to Joy"? Who can remain unmoved when a favorite love song is heard?

Songs have a way of piercing our very souls. They connect us with the deeper movements of our lives. In Scripture, when individuals felt God's presence—whether in joy or sorrow—they usually sang. When the Israelites, for example, marched through the Red Sea in dry sandals, they sang. When they were herded off into exile in Babylon, they sang. When the pregnant Mary visited her pregnant cousin Elizabeth, she sang.

Today we might ask ourselves: What role do songs play in my life—especially in my spiritual life? Which particular songs have the power to move me?

> God, give me a sense of your nearness today—
> whether in joy or in sorrow. Help me to keep
> singing!

16. *The Humor of Children*

One thing I always say to the people who attend my retreats or parish missions is this: Hang on to your sense of humor! Here are a few stories that might make you do just that:

Little Josh ran into the house after school and excitedly announced to his mother that he had won a prize in the first grade. After telling him how proud she was of him, his mother asked him what the prize was for. He replied, "I won for having the oldest mom in the whole class!"

Three little sisters spent most of the day fighting with each other. At two o'clock in the morning they were awakened by a terrible thunderstorm. Hearing an unusual noise upstairs, their father called up to them and asked what was going on. He heard a little voice say, "We're all in the closet forgiving each other."

On the first day of school, a father asked his first-grade son, "What does your new teacher look like?" The little boy replied, "Just like my kindergarten teacher—only with a different head."

After putting on some weight, a woman told her family she would be wearing a one-piece bathing suit instead of her usual two-piece suit. Her five-year-old son was shocked. He asked, "Which piece are you going to wear, Mom?"

A little boy's letter to God: "Dear God, My grandpa says you were around when he was a little boy. How far back do you go?"

God, our loving Father/Mother, thank you for the gift of children.

17. *Writing Begets Writing*

Writing begets writing. That's something I learned a long time ago. Some days I don't feel like writing. I say to myself, "I have nothing to say today." But instead of not writing, I sit down and begin to write—something, anything. For it's been my experience that writing leads to more writing. That is, the actual writing process draws forth words and ideas I didn't know were inside of me. Writing begets writing.

I've noticed that some other things work the same way. You don't feel like praying? Then pray—no matter how awkwardly or blandly. Just pray. Praying begets praying. Here are a few more "begets" on my list—both positive things and negative things: Love begets love...lies beget lies...trust begets trust...calm begets calm...anxiety begets anxiety...laughter begets laughter...good begets good...evil begets evil...fear begets fear...tenderness begets tenderness...hope begets hope.

It is important, then, that we choose carefully what we do, for behaviors have a tendency to beget more of the same.

Source of all goodness, beget in me more faith, hope, and love.

18. *Friendship with Jesus*

The third-grade teacher had her children write letters to Jesus, asking him whatever question they wanted to ask. One little boy wrote this: "Dear Jesus, Are you a good friend of Father Mike's or do you just know him through business?"

That's a good question—and one we should ask about ourselves. Are we a good friend of Jesus' or do we just know him through business? Is he a confidant or a mere acquaintance?

As we all know, there is a big difference between knowing *about* Jesus and *knowing Jesus.* In the first instance we may read about Jesus, study his words, and listen to what others say about him. We may eventually come to know all kinds of details about him and even become an expert on his life and teachings. But that's not the same as *knowing Jesus.* We come to know Jesus only by going directly to him, by speaking with him, by listening to him—in short, by establishing a personal relationship with him.

Pope Benedict XVI has written: "A mature adult faith is deeply rooted in friendship with Christ." How mature is my faith? How much is Jesus my friend?

Jesus, deepen my personal friendship with you.

19. *Quotations on Leadership*

"Leadership is more an art, a belief, a condition of the heart, than a set of things to do." • *Max De Pree*

"A leader takes people where they want to go. A great leader takes people where they don't want to go, but ought to be."
• *Rosalynn Carter*

"A leader is a dealer in hope." • *Napoleon Bonaparte*

"Effective [leadership] begins with the inability to leave well enough alone, with a preoccupation with betterment."
• *Priscilla Elfrey*

"If you aspire to leadership, take off your coat." • *Anonymous*

"Leaders don't create followers, they create more leaders."
• *Tom Peters*

Loving God, help me to be a better leader.

20. *Haunted by God*

I have given presentations titled "Seeking the Holy in Every Nook and Cranny." People tell me they come to such presentations because they are seeking to find God in their lives. I am quick to remind them that, although seeking God is certainly praiseworthy, we must always remember that God is always seeking us. In fact, God seeks us first!

Francis Thompson's beautiful poem "The Hound of Heaven" describes God as the Great Seeker. In fact, the poem goes so far as to compare God to a bloodhound that is hot on our trail. Nothing deters God from pursuing us. God comes after us relentlessly. The social activist Dorothy Day was fascinated by Eugene O'Neill's recitation of that poem when she heard it before her conversion to Christianity. She wrote, "The inevitability of the outcome made me feel that sooner or later I would have to pause in the mad rush of living and remember my first beginning and last end." The poem made her realize that "All my life I have been haunted by God."

The word "haunted" often has a negative connotation. But not in this context. God haunts us lovingly. God seeks us eagerly. God pursues us incessantly. The good news is: Sooner or later, in one way or another, God is going to get us.

*Seeker God, continue to haunt me no matter how
fast I may try to run away from you.*

21. Holy Doubt

Doubt does not cancel faith. It affirms faith's arduousness. It reminds us that faith is not easy, that it is often hard work. Doubt tells us that faith is not once-and-for-all, either. It is every-day-anew. Faith is not relaxation, but a constant struggle against discouragement and selfishness, a struggle that grants us no rest.

When doubts about my faith arise in me, I try not to panic. I don't immediately assume, for example, that I am losing my faith. Instead, I look upon doubts as a chance to revisit my beliefs so that my faith may grow and mature. I try to be more at ease with uncertainties and mystery without reaching for quick answers or pious solutions. Doubts enable faith to grow. And faith must grow, for yesterday's faith is insufficient for today's needs.

Kenneth Leech, an Anglican priest, says that true faith "includes the elements of paradox and creative doubt." He adds, "For faith in God does not bring the false peace of answered questions and resolved paradoxes."

Spiritual writer Robert Wicks says that sometimes the amount of trust we have in God is best measured "by the depth of the doubt and the seriousness of the questions with which we are willing to live." Another spiritual writer, Frederick Buechner, puts it more humorously. He claims, when it comes to faith, "if you don't have any doubts you are either kidding yourself or asleep." He adds, "Doubts are the ants in the pants of faith. They keep it awake and moving."

God of paradox and mystery, may all my doubts enable my faith in you to grow and mature.

22. *The Mystery of the Shrinking Teddy Bear*

My nephew Chris and his wife, Stacey, recently had a little boy they named Reece. Since he is their first child, Chris and Stacey regularly e-mail pictures of him to us relatives. One set of pictures was especially creative. Labeled "The Mystery of the Shrinking Teddy Bear," the two pictures showed Reece lying on the floor next to a white teddy bear. In the first picture, taken when Reece was one month old, he is a little smaller than the bear. But in the next picture, taken at four months, Reece is already noticeably bigger than the bear. Using the teddy bear was a unique way to measure their baby's growth.

But how do we measure our spiritual growth? One way can be by the books we read. Sometimes I pick up a spiritual book that I really enjoyed when I was much younger. As I read it again, twenty or thirty years later, the book falls flat. It no longer speaks to me the way it did when I was younger. Or the opposite can happen. I pick up a book I didn't particularly care for twenty or thirty years ago, only to find that it suddenly touches my soul deeply. In both instances, the book is the same as it was many years ago. But *I* am not the same. *I* have grown over the years—hopefully for the better.

We can measure our spiritual growth in other ways, too. Perhaps we fret less often than we used to. Or maybe we reach out to others more easily or naturally. Or we laugh more regularly, live more simply, and are more sensitive to the feelings of others.

God of growth, teach me to measure my spiritual growth against the backdrop of your love and goodness to me.

23. *Something Is Asked of Me*

Moses was tending sheep when he spotted a burning bush. Curious, he went closer to investigate the phenomenon. Suddenly, God called out to him from the bush, eventually entrusting him with a mission: "I will send you to Pharaoh to lead my people, the Israelites, out of Egypt" (Ex 3:10).

Such a task was certainly a daunting one. No wonder Moses protested, "Who am I that I should go to Pharaoh and lead the Israelites out of Egypt?" (Ex 3:11). But God tried to ease his fears with this promise, "I will be with you" (3:12).

A great Jewish writer, Rabbi Abraham Heschel, wrote: "This is the most important experience in the life of every human being: *something is asked of me.*" This occurs when we first realize that the gifts of life are meant to be shared and not hoarded. Just as God asked something of Moses, so, too, does God ask things of us: "Love your children...Be faithful to your spouse...Care for your elderly parents...Share your goods with the less fortunate...Visit that lonely neighbor...Encourage the disheartened...Work for peace and justice...Be honest in all you do."

Sometimes our particular mission may seem next to impossible, and we wonder how we will ever carry it out. Perhaps we have a difficult position of leadership. Or we were recently diagnosed with a serious chronic illness. Or maybe we have lost a loved one and can't imagine living without that person. Or perhaps we are carrying the wounds of abuse or addiction. It is then that we must recall the words God spoke to Moses long ago, for they are the same words God speaks to us today: "I will be with you."

God the Great Sender, help me to carry out the missions you ask of me, keeping always in mind that you are with me.

24. *"All Summer in a Day"*

"All Summer in a Day" is a short story by Ray Bradbury. I used to love reading it with my high school students. It is a science fiction story that tells of a group of nine-year-old schoolchildren living in an underground city on Venus. They are the children of space travelers from Earth who came to colonize the dark, cold, wet planet.

In Bradbury's story, it constantly rains on Venus. In fact, the sun appears only once every seven years and only for one hour. One of the children, Margot, moved from Earth to Venus only five years before the story takes place. She is a frail child who looks as if "she had been lost in the rain for years." The other children are jealous of Margot because she remembers the sun on Earth and writes poems about it.

One day, when the teacher leaves the room, the children lock Margot in the closet. Shortly afterward, the teacher comes back and eagerly leads the children outside to see the sun. In their excitement and joy, they forget about Margot. Once outside, they play and dance in the sun until the thunder and returning rain chase them back inside and underground.

Back in the classroom, the children suddenly remember Margot. Horrified by what they have done, they slowly walk over to the closet, open the door, and let Margot out. The resplendent sun has come and gone for seven more years, but poor little Margot never got the chance to see it.

The story is a commentary on jealousy and the cruelty of children, yes. But for me, it is much more than that. It is a magnificent paean to the sun. Bradbury describes the dark, wet existence on Venus so effectively that when the sun finally appears, the reader feels as excited and astonished by its beauty as the children in the story. The story always reminds me never to take for granted any aspect of God's splendid creation.

Creator of all, I thank you for the sun and for every other aspect of your beautiful creation.

25. Why Is There So Much Goodness?

M. Scott Peck, a well-known writer and psychologist, once said that throughout his thirty years of practice, many people asked him, "Why is there so much evil in the world?" During those same thirty years, not one person ever asked him, "Why is there so much good in the world?"

He makes an interesting observation. Why do we tend to be fixated on evil rather than good? Why are we more apt to harp on what's wrong with the world than with what's right with the world? Why do our newspapers focus on vice rather than virtue, on corruption rather than integrity, on the criminal rather than the person of integrity?

Instead of asking why so many people are so crabby, so selfish, so bent on doing evil things, maybe we should be asking, why are so many people so pleasant, so kind, so devoted to doing good things? If we could get at the bottom of the mystery of goodness, we could change the world.

To do this we must begin with changing our perspective. Although we must not deny or ignore all that is wrong in the world, we must not be overwhelmed by the evil that we see, that we hear, and (to be honest) that we contribute to. We must balance the realization of evil with the appreciation of all the good and the beautiful that surround us each day. And we must be quick to talk about the goodness we experience in our families, workplaces, neighborhoods, parishes, and larger communities. Pope John Paul II wrote in *Crossing the Threshold of Faith*, "Good is greater than all that is evil in the world." Do we believe that?

Good and Gracious God, help me to focus on all that is right with my particular world and with the larger world.

FALL

"Delicious autumn! My very soul is wedded to it, and if I were a bird I would fly about the earth seeking successive autumns."

GEORGE ELIOT

26. *Earth Tilts*

Earth tilts. She leans 23.4 degrees on her axis. In his book *My Story as Told by Water*, David James Duncan describes Planet Earth in these words: "...like a long-ago-injured woman who's learned to walk gracefully with a cane, Earth leans ever so slightly on her axis, inclining now toward the sun, now away from it as she orbits, thereby causing the angle at which sunlight strikes her to change constantly."

In places like northeastern Ohio, where I live, it is impossible to forget Earth's tilt, for it results in four dramatically different seasons. We go from hot, humid days in summer with temperatures in the 90s to cold, snowy days in winter with temperatures below zero. Earth's tilt is thus responsible for the annual cycle of growth, fruition, death, and dormancy of plant life. It also causes the migration of countless species of wildlife.

Migration is essential for many birds and animals. As the tilt of the sun makes their summer homes inhospitable, they must discover and trace a path to more life-sustaining environs. Thus wildlife of all kinds migrate: The phalarope flies from the Arctic Circle to the equator each year, while the Arctic tern flies from pole to pole. The wildebeest and caribou trek thousands of miles across vast plains, while the seal and humpback whale swim a lengthy marathon in the ocean. A host of human beings also join this vast migration, as they journey to warmer climes for the winter months.

In one sense, though, the life forms that migrate do not move at all. As Duncan notes, "it is the so-called 'migratory' mammals and birds that travel thousands of miles north and south who *maintain their true solar place.*" It is those of us who stay put all year long who are the real travelers, as each year Earth swishes us into a new relationship to the sun. We may look stationary, but that's an illusion. We're moving! We're being swept away! Not only ourselves, but everything around us that appears to be stationary is moving, too: our house, the trees, our town, our rivers, our hills and mountains. We're all sailing together to a new solar place—all because our dear Planet Earth tilts.

For me, fall is the time of the year I am most aware that my place in the sun is changing dramatically. As the days shorten, as the sun moves farther south on the horizon, as frost appears on the pumpkins, as the leaves turn vivid colors and begin to fall, I sense I am indeed moving. I feel I am being carried into winter—often against my will. I am being helplessly swept into a time of cold, darkness, apparent death, and dormancy. This dramatic shift makes me a little sad and melancholic. Yet, I remind myself, if I hang on through the cold and darkness, I will, at the time of the winter solstice, begin my glide back into spring again.

God of all seasons, be with me in all the sweeping changes of my life.

27. *Our Hope Lies in* _____

Ask people on the street to finish this sentence:

Our hope lies in _____.

What might they say? Our hope lies in: financial security, capitalism, free enterprise, democracy, our legal system, our ingenuity, our willingness to work hard, a particular leader. But for us Christians, there is only one word that can truly complete that sentence: Our hope lies in Jesus.

Sometimes, however, even we believers live as if our hope lies elsewhere. We live as if our hope lies in our goodness or our fidelity, and thus we become disheartened when we fall short of our ideals or when we sin. Or we act as if our hope lies in our intelligence and cleverness, and we become discouraged when we see no way out of the mess we are in or our world is in. Or we live as if our hope lies in a particular pope, pastor, or other church leader, and we are despondent when our leaders fall short of the virtue we expect of them. Or we live as if our hope lies in a particular program, a certain way of doing liturgy, or a new way of praying, and we are saddened when these don't produce the effects we had hoped for.

No. Repeat after me: Our hope lies in Jesus. *In Jesus.* Period. Amen. Alleluia!

My hope lies in you, Jesus. Only you. Alleluia!

28. *Meditation on an Apple*

(As you read this reflection, it's best if you have an actual apple in your hand.)

Behold the apple! Behold this particular apple you have in your hand. Begin your beholding by noticing your apple's color. Is it red, green, yellow, reddish pink, greenish red, burgundy, or some other color? Is its skin smooth or rough? Do you notice any so-called imperfections such as bumps, holes, soft spots, bruises? How do you suppose they got there?

Do you know the kind of apple you have in your hand? Is it, for example, a Red Delicious, Yellow Delicious, McIntosh, Jonathan, Fuji, Gala, Granny Smith, or something else? Do you know where your apple came from? Was it grown locally or did it travel great distances to reach your hand? Even if your apple was grown in your own backyard, it has traveled vast distances to get to you, for all apples trace their origin to the northern slopes of the Tien Shan Mountains, what is now the border between China and Kazakhstan.

Apple trees must be pruned regularly. Entire branches must be snipped off in order to concentrate the tree's nutrients into fewer but bigger and better apples. Apple trees also must be cross-pollinated to produce fruit. Growers rely on bees to do this important task.

If you cut your apple horizontally, you will find inside a five-pointed star. Inside each ray of the star are the seeds—usually two or three per ray. Apple seeds are mildly poisonous. Although they won't hurt humans, they do deter birds. Most apple trees are not grown from seeds, however, because seedling apple trees often differ greatly from their parent trees. Most apple trees are produced by grafting.

Apple trees are prolific. A single tree produces between 80 to 440 pounds of fruit a year! Sometimes the branches of the tree are so heavy with fruit, they must be shored up or they will actually break.

The old proverb says: An apple a day keeps the doctor away. Apples have been shown to reduce the risk of certain kinds of cancer. They also contain fiber and are good for the digestive tract. And apples have no cholesterol, so they're healthy to eat.

Take one final look at your apple....Bite into it or cut off a piece and eat it...Is your apple sweet, tart, or somewhere in between? Is it juicy or dry? If you are inclined, continue to eat your apple. But as you do, thank God for this precious gift. And thank God for the many lessons apples teach us: lessons about variety, pruning, cross-pollination, and fruitfulness.

God of all fruitfulness, I thank you for all the ordinary blessings in my life.

29. Saints and Work

Brother Michael O'Neill McGrath, an artist, has produced several books about the saints. His first one, *Occupations: Patrons and Protectors*, contains his images of twenty-eight saints as patrons of particular occupations. Among the saints and occupations included in the book are the following: St. Peter (fishermen), St. Isidore (farmers), St. Margaret Clitherow (businesswomen), St. Joan of Arc (military personnel), St. Ann (homemakers), St. John Baptist de la Salle (teachers), St. Matthew (bankers and accountants), St. Frances Cabrini (hospital administrators), St. Thomas More (lawyers), and St. Thérèse of Lisieux (airplane pilots).

The illustrations are both imaginative and instructive. Each one is accompanied by a brief narrative about the saint as well as an essay by contemporary men and women engaged in that particular occupation. The book makes the saints come alive. It reminds us that before the saints were reduced to granite statues or stilted portraits, they were real men and women actively engaged in a wide variety of labors in their quest to bring about God's reign on earth. The saints achieved holiness not despite their work, but precisely in and through their work.

A book such as this helps us to see our work as integral to our lives as Christians. We come to see the connection between our work and God's work. Everything we do—whether answering the phone, waiting on a customer, wringing out a mop, typing at a computer, talking with a child, sitting at a meeting—can be part of how we are bringing about the reign of God on earth. Through our labors, we become co-creators with God. Through our work, we are sanctified.

Creator God, bless the work of my hands today and always.

30. *The Individual and the Community*

Confucianism sees human beings as embedded in concentric circles of relations: family, society, the nation, and the earth itself. It stresses the interconnection of humans with everyone and everything else. The Western world, in contrast, tends to focus on individualism, the rights of each single person.

Perhaps the best view would be a blending of the two, a view that combines the intrinsic value of community with the intrinsic value of the individual.

Isn't this precisely what Jesus did? Didn't he blend these two views?

Jesus loved and respected individuals. He took the blind man away from the crowd, for example, to heal him. He conversed with Nicodemus one-on-one. He told a parable about a shepherd who leaves ninety-nine sheep in order to rescue just one. The number one was a precious number for Jesus.

At the same time, Jesus valued community. He commanded that we individuals love one another. He taught us the way to form and nourish community—through love, patience, humility, and forgiveness. He constantly called people to come together in community. In his parables, he said the kingdom of God was like a wedding reception, a gathering together of individuals to celebrate family and love, to enjoy each other's company.

A question to ask myself regularly: How am I balancing individualism and community in my life right now?

Jesus, help me to balance my respect for individuals with my need for community.

31. *Walking*

I love to walk. Ordinarily I try to walk a mile or two each day. Sometimes I go to the nearby park. Other times I roam the neighborhood. In bad weather I seek out a mall or (on non-school days) the hallways of our parish school. If I'm really desperate, I use the treadmill down in the basement. I walk for the exercise, true. But I also walk because something happens to me when I walk—especially when I walk by myself.

If I'm walking outside, I find myself spontaneously observing nature. I notice the slant of the sunlight, the particular color of the sky. I spot wildlife—whether a cluster of geese on the pond, a squirrel scurrying along the ground, or a red-tailed hawk perched in the upper branches of a dead tree. A walk outside forces me to break out of myself, my puny world, my preoccupation with my own concerns and worries. It puts me in touch with a larger world. It underscores my place in the greater scheme of things.

Walking also slows me down. It encourages reflection and even conversation. When I walk, I find myself effortlessly talking to God. Sometimes my words are few—a mere "Thank you!...What a gorgeous day, God!" Sometimes my words are lengthier. I tell God how I feel, where I am, what's on my mind, what's in my heart. Walking and praying naturally go together for me.

As a walker, I am one with a host of other individuals (some of them quite famous) who loved to walk and did so regularly. Henry David Thoreau walked several miles each day, just for the sheer pleasure of it. He remarked, "It's a great art to saunter." The Chinese philosopher Lao Tzu said, "Meandering leads to perfection." Saint Jerome wrote, "*Solvitur ambulando*"—"To solve a problem, walk around." Writer and poet Jacqueline Schiff gave us yet another reason to walk when she said, "The best remedy for a short temper is a long walk." Author Raymond Inmon wrote, "If you are seeking creative ideas, go out walking. Angels whisper to us when we go for a walk."

If there ever comes a day when I can no longer walk, I hope to God someone will be there to get me into a wheelchair and push me outside for a nice long "walk."

Loving God, give me a greater appreciation for walking, sauntering, and meandering.

32. *The Birth of a Panda*

On TV a while back, I watched a show about the birth of a panda at the National Zoo. This birth was the cause of immense celebration, for it was the first panda birth at the zoo after thirty years of trying!

It seems pandas, for some unknown reason, lose their interest in mating once they're in captivity. Some scientists have resorted to extreme measures to encourage pandas to become amorous. They show them videos of other pandas mating or they give male pandas Viagra. This particular baby panda, like most in captivity, was conceived through artificial insemination.

A video camera in the mother panda's cage caught the birth on film. When the baby was born, it "shot out" of its mother, hitting a cement wall in the process. Zoo personnel feared that the baby might have been injured during the birth, but they would not be able to actually examine the baby for several weeks.

Baby pandas weigh only 3.2 to 4.6 ounces when they are born—"about the size of a stick of butter," said the narrator of the film. They are born pink, furless, and blind. In fact, they are so helpless, they demand their mother's undivided attention. This particular mother panda never left her baby's side—even to eat. This is not unusual. Mother pandas often go thirty days or even more without food after they give birth.

Twenty-five days after this little cub was born, the zoo personnel coaxed the mother out of her cage to eat. While she ate in another room, they sneaked into the cage and took her cub. They quickly examined it, concluding it was a boy and basically healthy. They weighed it (one pound, eight ounces) and promptly returned it to the cage. As they did this, the baby panda squeaked a few times. As soon as the mother heard the squeaking, she left the food and hurried back into the cage to care for her cub.

God of all, may I reverence and learn from the mystery of every living being.

33. September 8: Mary's Birthday

On September 8, we celebrate Mary's birthday. No one really knows what day Mary was born, of course. All we do know is that September 8 is exactly nine months after December 8, the feast of the Immaculate Conception. The planners of the liturgical calendar reasoned, if we celebrate Mary's conception on December 8, then we should celebrate her birthday on September 8, and vice versa. That makes sense—at least biologically speaking.

The truth is, who cares what date we use? The date of Mary's birth is not important. The way she lived her life is! That's what we really celebrate on September 8. And how did Mary live her life? By believing in a God who was active and alive in the history of her people and in her own personal history. By experiencing this God as a God of love. By communing with this God daily in prayer. By trusting this God to do surprising and seemingly impossible things. By risking her reputation in God's name. By entrusting her uncertain future completely into God's hands. By doing well and with love all the ordinary tasks involved in marriage and motherhood. This is what we celebrate on September 8—not simply Mary's birthday, but Mary's life.

Mary, thank you for the beautiful example of your life. Help me to make my life worth celebrating, too.

34. As Others See Us

I was giving a retreat day for a faculty of a Catholic elementary school near where I live. Posted on the walls of the large room in which we were gathered were pictures that the younger children had drawn of their teachers. Many of the drawings evoked smiles in the teachers as they saw how their children viewed them. One unusual thing we noticed in nearly all the portraits was that the teachers had large nostrils. We soon figured out why: When little children look up at their teachers, the nostrils are very prominent. The children were just drawing what they saw—from their angle!

Another time, I was giving a mission in a small parish. I spoke at all the Masses on Sunday and then gave a presentation on three consecutive evenings. One little girl, Aubrey, about ten, was present at all my talks. At the end of the mission, she presented me with a drawing she had made of me. I had to smile because it really did look like me. She got the hair right, the glasses, the crucifix, the plaid blazer. She even got the two chins right. She also drew me smiling and my eyes sparkling.

But what I appreciated the most about her portrait were the items she placed around me, items she apparently associated with me: a cross, a chalice, a host, a candle, and the words "Bless the Lord." I thought, "Yes, those items are pretty much the real essentials of my life." I keep Aubrey's picture on my desk. I hope to live up to the way she drew me. Sometimes it can be helpful to find out how others see us.

🌿 *Divine Artist, help me to see myself as* you *see me.*

35. *Jesus Is a Thief in the Night*

Once I saw a TV newscast which featured two reformed burglars who demonstrated for the camera their finely tuned burglary skills. They broke into a house, snatched up significant valuables, and drove off—all within a matter of a few minutes. These professional thieves were sneaky, fast, and selective. They made a good living stealing other people's valuables.

Jesus once compared himself to a thief in the night. He said,

"Be sure of this: if the master of the house had known the hour of the night when the thief was coming, he would have stayed awake and not let his house be broken into. So too, you must be prepared, for at an hour you do not expect, the Son of Man will come." • *Matthew 24:43–44*

The image is a little shocking. Jesus a burglar? The idea may even seem sacrilegious. But in another way, the image is very appropriate. For Jesus is good at breaking and entering our lives—often when we least expect it. He is not deterred by the defenses we sometimes build to keep him out—busyness, pride, preoccupation with material things. Jesus comes like a thief in the night—"burglarizing" our neat little houses, stealing our hearts, and conning us into selfless loving.

Jesus, help me to stay awake to welcome you into my house today.

36. *"Poet and Peasant Overture"*

I was sitting at the drive-through window at the bank when my car radio started playing Franz von Suppé's "Poet and Peasant Overture." Instantly my eyes filled with tears. It took my brain several seconds to figure out why I was crying. "Poet and Peasant" was one of my deceased father's favorite classical pieces. He played it over and over again when I was growing up. Just hearing those opening strains brought tears to my eyes, confirming how much I still missed Dad, although he had been dead for almost a year. The tears also confirmed how much I still loved him. Along with my tears, I felt a deep inner peace as I continued to listen to that beautiful overture all the way home. I felt as if my father was somehow in the car with me, assuring me of his love.

Tears and peace. Pain and love. We sometimes think they are mutually exclusive. But more often than not, tears and pain are merely the flip side of peace and love.

God of consolation, open my ears to hear the ways you are assuring me of your love today.

37. *Freed from Prison*

In Acts, we read how an angel of the Lord freed the disciples from prison. As he led them to freedom, the angel said, "Go and take your place in the temple area, and tell the people everything about this life" (5:20).

Notice, he didn't send them home. He didn't say, "Go and hide somewhere so they won't catch you again." No, the angel sent them right back to the temple area and told them to continue their preaching of the Gospel—the very thing that had landed them in jail in the first place. This passage is noteworthy. It reminds us that being Christian is not about being safe.

We, too, have been set free by God's Spirit, in different ways. Perhaps we have been freed from addiction, ignorance, fear, poverty, illness, despair. If so, we must remember that we have been freed not to retreat into our own secure little world. We have been freed to go out into the world and preach the good news. And we don't have to go very far, either. We can preach the good news in our own home, at our workplace, in our parish or neighborhood. And we preach the good news not by giving lectures about it, but by living it.

Spirit of God, free me from whatever imprisons me.
Then send me forth to preach and live the good news.

38. *I Am Not Alone*

I decide to drive to the park and go for a walk. It is a lovely late morning in early September. As I pull into the parking lot, I notice there are no other cars around. I walk across the wooden bridge that leads to the path that goes around the lake. Before I set off, I pause and scan the area. I see no one—no one walking a dog, no one jogging, no one fishing from one of the docks. "I'm alone!" I say with excitement. "All alone!"

But as soon as I utter those words, I smile. Although I may be the only *human being* in the park this morning, I am certainly not alone! I am not the only *being*. There are countless other living beings with me in the park—for example, the birds I see flying around—a few sparrows, goldfinches, and swallows. I spot a couple of ducks swimming along the shore of the lake and a group of geese sitting out in the middle holding some kind of a meeting. I see bees busily visiting the small white flowers growing along the path. I hear the steady hum of the cicadas from the trees and underbrush. And I'm startled by a couple of grasshoppers—masters of the broad jump—who show off their incredible athletic ability for me as I walk along the path.

And what about all the living things I don't see? The bluegills and bass in the lake. The large turtle I've seen on occasion who I know calls this lake home. Then there's the brown and white snake I spotted a few weeks ago skimming the water along the shore. And don't forget the elusive deer, the squirrels, rabbits, and raccoons, and the bats that are probably hanging upside down asleep in the bat house that the park rangers erected for them. And how could I forget all the worms, beetles, snails, slugs, and other small creatures hiding in the grass or burrowing beneath the ground? And let's not forget the *flora*—the bushes of all kinds and the trees—the willows, oaks, dogwoods, and maples with their leaves already turning orange and brown.

No, I am not alone. There are thousands of other living things here with me today in this park. And why should I limit companionship to only living things? What about all the so-called inanimate things that are with me as I walk—the earth I tread upon, the rocks along the shore of the lake, the sun and clouds above me, the air I breathe as I walk, and the beautiful lake itself. Aren't these all beings, too?

My realization today as I walked alone in the park: I am not alone. Ever.

Companion God, make me more aware today of all the beings who accompany me as I walk through life.

39. *Where Do We Aim Our Cameras?*

When I watch a football game on TV, I am amazed at the number of photographers lined up along the sidelines and behind the end zones. On every play of the game, they aim their cameras toward the action on the field, hoping to catch an exciting picture. Sure enough, in the next day's newspaper there it is—a great shot of a receiver making an incredible catch, a quarterback being sacked, a player rushing for a key first down.

But as I see those photographers lined up and vying for the best shot, I can't help but think that it's "overkill," and, in one way, a waste of film and talent. All that attention focused on a game! It makes me ask: Aren't there other, more important things you should be photographing? What pictures does the world *really* need to see?

I believe we need to see more pictures of people who need our help, and of people doing good things—even if those things aren't very exciting. Perhaps we need more photographers taking pictures of the homeless living under our city bridges…a man and woman celebrating their sixty-fifth wedding anniversary…malnourished children in East Africa…a meeting at the United Nations to discuss relief for victims of AIDS…a third-grade teacher walking into school in the morning, eager and well-prepared….a scientist bent over a telescope in a lab in search of a cure for some disease.

The photographers at a football game raise the question for me: What are we as a community focusing on? What are we overlooking? Similarly, I ask myself: What gets my personal attention? What am I overlooking?

Loving God, draw my attention to someone in need and someone doing good things.

40. *The Burning Bush*

The house next door has a large "burning bush" (a kind of deciduous shrub) in the front yard. This bush is green most of the year, but in autumn its leaves turn a brilliant red before they fall. The bush is a magnificent sight to behold. I look forward to witnessing its amazing transformation each fall.

I had a friend who turned her small backyard into a verdant garden. I asked her once if she had ever considered planting a burning bush in her garden. She said she had but decided against it. "Fifty weeks of ordinariness for a two-week splurge in color? I didn't think it was worth it."

She had a point—especially considering her limited space. At the same time, though, her answer made me wonder: What is the ratio of the ordinary to the extraordinary in my life? Like the burning bush, is my life about fifty parts ordinary to two parts extraordinary? I'm not sure, but this I do know: I am sometimes too quick to label things as ordinary and thus miss out on their true extraordinariness.

Take the burning bush. Why should I limit my appreciation of this shrub to the brief time it is brilliant red? Why can't I appreciate it all year long—when it is a mass of lush green leaves, and even when its lack of leaves allows me to see the intricate structure of its branches?

God of the ordinary and extraordinary, give me a greater appreciation of everything.

41. *Whom Do Atheists Thank?*

The author F. Scott Fitzgerald once wrote that although he never desired a God to pray to, he often desired a God to thank. The great English writer G.K. Chesterton was raised without religion. He claimed he found his way to faith in God as an adult because he needed someone to be grateful to. I resonate with these stories, for I believe that faith can begin with the desire to thank someone for life's obvious blessings.

What kind of blessings? The birth of a healthy baby...the beauty of a sunset...the endurance of a good friendship...the recovery from an illness...the resolving of a conflict...the nourishment of a good meal...the laughter over a funny story...the song of a wren…the success of an important venture…the presence of clean air to breathe.

Gratitude has the power not only to lead us to faith but also to transform our lives. As psychologist Melody Beattie writes, "Gratitude…can turn a meal into a feast, a house into a home, a stranger into a friend."

Whom do I thank for life's blessings? How? How often? Has gratitude transformed my life in any way?

Giver of all good gifts, thank you, thank you.

42. *The Parking Space*

A man was driving down the street frantically looking for a parking space because he had an important meeting. But all the spaces were taken. In desperation, the man looked up to heaven and prayed, "God, if you find me a parking space, I promise to go to church every Sunday and give up swearing for the rest of my life." Suddenly a parking space opened up right in front of him. The man looked up and said, "Never mind, God. I found one."

I love this little story. First of all, it reminds me that when we're in trouble or in need of something, we naturally turn to God. If only we would turn to God whether we're in trouble or not! The story also says that sometimes we even bargain with God: "If you do this, God, I promise to do that." If we resort to bargaining, it is often hard to keep our part of the bargain—especially if it entails changing our lives.

I am not advocating that we bargain with God. After all, God is someone to be loved, not bargained with. There's a big difference. If we bargain with God, we're using the promise of good behavior to get something we want from God. But if we truly love God, we trust God enough to give us all we really need in life. Our good behavior, then, is never a bribe. It is the natural result of knowing how much we are already loved by God. We do not make friendship with God contingent on God's doing small favors for us, for God has already done the "inconceivable favor" of loving us into existence and loving us forever.

God, make me more aware of your inconceivable love for me.

43. *The Wonder of Healing*

I burned myself two weeks ago on my left wrist. I was taking a casserole out of the oven and I brushed my wrist against one of the upper coils in the oven. Ouch! Although the burn hurt for a bit, it soon became little more than a minor distraction. But what I enjoyed doing these past two weeks was observing the healing process of that burn.

I did nothing to facilitate the healing—no cream or medication. I did transfer my watch to my right wrist so it wouldn't rub against the burn, but other than that, I did nothing. The healing occurred on its own. Each day I checked the condition of the burn and was fascinated by what I saw. I watched as the scab formed, as it began to itch, and as it eventually fell off, revealing smooth pink skin beneath. Right now there is only a pale pinkish line where the burn had been. That, too, will fade in time, until there will probably be no sign at all of the burn. Incredible! What magic!

The healing process is one of the body's greatest mysteries. It's also one of life's greatest gifts. Writer John Updike has even written a poem, titled "Ode to Healing," about this gift. He says, "A scab is a beautiful thing—a coin the body has minted with an invisible motto: In God We Trust." The healing of my small burn gave me the impetus to reflect on these questions: How appreciative am I of the healing process—and other wonders of the human body? How patient am I with the healing process? What other healings am I in need of—whether of body or soul?

Masterful Creator, I thank you for the power of healing you have invested in the human body, psyche, and soul.

44. *Quotations about God*

"Nothing is far from God." ◦ *St. Monica*

"People learn about God from Godlike people."
◦ *William Bausch*

"To most, even good people, God is a belief. To the saints, God is an embrace." ◦ *Francis Thompson*

"If we seek a God we can 'handle,' that will be exactly what we get. A God we can manipulate, suspiciously like ourselves, the wideness of whose mercy we've cut down to size."
◦ *Kathleen Norris*

"God is the Divine Mystery, not our Cosmic Pal." • *Mitch Finley*

"Isn't it the greatest possible disaster, when you are wrestling with God, not to be beaten?" • *Simone Weil*

"Whosoever walks toward God one cubit, God runs toward him twain." • *Anonymous*

God, continue to reveal to me who you really are.

45. The Bird Guard

As I strolled in the orchard on our provincial house property one fall day, I heard some birds chirping loudly. Curious, I began to search for them in the apple trees that surrounded me. I stepped slowly and cautiously so as not to scare them away. Imagine my surprise when I came upon a wooden pole in the middle of the orchard with four spokes on top sticking out in four directions. Attached to the end of each spoke was a small speaker. Wires ran down from the speakers to a metal box on the pole. The chirping sounds I heard were coming from those four speakers. The chirps weren't real. They were canned!

I laughed out loud as I walked closer to investigate the contraption. It's called a "Bird Guard." Evidently the chirping of the fake birds helps to keep real birds out of the orchard and deters them from eating all the apples, pears, and plums. Real birds are fooled into thinking that there are already many other birds in the orchard, so they move on. Printed on the metal box were settings for different kinds of bird chirps, as well as dials to regulate their frequency and intensity.

I shook my head, saying to myself, "How much does something like this cost? Does it really work?"

Later I visited several websites of companies that manufacture things to control "pesky birds." There are hundreds of products out there: guards for dryer and bathroom vents, chimney caps, repellents, and sound deterrents of all kinds, including ultrasonic devices. One category of deterrents was labeled "visual deterrents." It included a stuffed owl, a coyote decoy, and my favorite: a replica of an alligator head that floats in your pond and repels ducks, geese, and maybe even your neighbors!

As lovely as birds are, they can be pests at times. We humans have devised some ingenious ways of controlling them without harming them.

Creative God, help me to use my creativity to ease someone's need today.

46. *Finding Humor Everywhere*

"Only the mediocre are always at their best." ◆ *Jean Giraudoux*

"No matter what happens, somebody will find a way to take it too seriously." ◆ *Dave Barry*

A farewell message to a departing priest in a parish bulletin: "You will be forever in our thoughts and prayers. You leave with out respect and love."

"If it weren't for electricity, we'd be watching television by candlelight." ◆ *George Gobel*

"Some people are born on third base and go through life thinking they hit a triple." • *Barry Switzer*

Wife: "I'll admit I'm wrong if you'll admit I'm right."
Husband: "Okay. You go first."
Wife: "I'm wrong."
Husband: "You're right."

"Living on earth may be expensive, but it includes a free trip around the sun annually." • *Anonymous*

God, don't let me take life so seriously that I fail to see the humor all around me.

47. *I Want to Go Back, God*

Sometimes my prayer is, "I want to go back, God. I want to go back in time." I find myself saying this when I'm feeling melancholy, or when I'm missing my deceased loved ones, or when I feel left behind by the fast-paced and ever-changing times in which we live.

I want to go back, I say to God. I want to go back to my childhood on the farm, to my early days in school, to my first years in religious life when I often felt so close to God, to my days in the classroom when I was young, energetic, creative, and so devoted to my teaching. I want to go back to a time when I felt more at home in the world, more in sync with my neighbors and fellow countrymen, a time when things weren't so frantic, confusing, and scary.

But even as I say these words, I know I can't go back. I know that life—real life—lies before me, not behind me. And I know that God is calling me to move forward into the future—just as God called Abraham to leave the familiarity of Ur and journey to a land he knew not, just as God called the Israelites out of Egypt, into the desert, and into the Promised Land, just as God called Mary not to remain a little girl, but to become the mother of "the Son of the Most High."

In truth, my deceased loved ones were not left behind when they died—although it may seem like they were. No, my loved ones went on ahead of me when they died. They stand before me—on the brink of my future—beckoning me, encouraging me, waiting for me. Believing this, I pray these words instead: There are times I want to go back, God. But don't let me give in to the temptation to forsake the journey, the journey of my particular life. Don't let me turn back and live in the past. Instead, help me to keep walking forward. Remind me that every step into the future is one step closer to the fullness of who you are. Amen.

God of the journey, keep me moving forward.

48. *The Flying Trapeze Artist*

The priest and popular spiritual writer Henri Nouwen was fascinated with the circus. He eventually became friends with the Flying Rodleighs, a troupe of trapeze artists. In their artistry, Nouwen found a number of images for the spiritual life.

For example, one of the trapeze artists explained that in their act there were flyers and catchers. He told Nouwen that during their performance, the flyer did nothing really. It was the catcher who did all the work. Said the man, "When I fly to the catcher, I have simply to stretch out my arms and hands and wait for him to catch me. The flyer must trust with outstretched arms that his catcher will be there for him."

Nouwen saw a parallel in the spiritual life. We are the flyer; God is the catcher. Nouwen concluded that our identity and success are not measured by how much we stay in control, but by how much we are able to trust, let go, and place ourselves into the hands of the Divine Catcher.

Divine Catcher, as I fly to you, teach me to stretch out my arms and hands, trusting that you will catch me.

49. *Waiting and Watching*

As a child, I often saw my mother waiting and watching for my father. He worked long hours, often not coming home until 8:00 or so in the evening. Mom and we kids ate our supper at 6:00. After we had eaten and done the dishes, Mom went into her bedroom and sat on the side of her bed looking out the west window. She sat there watching for our green Packard to come down the road. As soon as Mom spotted it, she hopped up and announced, "Dad's coming," and hurried into the kitchen to get his supper on the table for him. This was her evening ritual.

My mother also performed a morning ritual every day as my father left for work, usually in the darkness. We had a small light on our side porch. After kissing my mother goodbye, my father walked all the way back to the garage to get the car. As he drove out our long driveway, he had to pass by the side porch. Mom waited and watched for him and, as he passed by, she flicked the porch light on and off a few times, signaling her goodbye to the man she loved.

From my mother I learned this great truth: Love watches and waits. It is not content just to *be* with the loved one. It anticipates the arrival of the loved one by keeping vigil. Love also marks the departure of the loved one with little rituals—that is, with special signs of affection.

In the parable of the prodigal son, we read that while the wayward son "was still a long way off, his father caught sight of him" (Lk 15:20). How could the father have seen his son at a distance unless he was watching for him?

For whom have I watched and waited? Does anyone watch and wait for me?

God, may I watch and wait for the loved ones in my life just as you watch and wait for me.

50. *A Tap on the Shoulder*

As you may know, two years ago I was diagnosed with a rare illness called polymyositis. It is an autoimmune disorder that causes the immune system to attack the muscles in the body. There is no known cause and no cure, but medication can manage the disease for some people. When I was first diagnosed, I experienced considerable pain, stiffness, and fatigue.

I didn't know if I would respond to the medications or not. I heard that twenty percent of the people with polymyositis die within five years. Would I be in that group?

Fortunately, after several months I began to respond to the medication, and I am doing quite well now. But this serious illness forced me to face my potential paralysis and even my possible imminent death. I was talking to a friend of mine recently and she remarked, "Your polymyositis was a tap on the shoulder for you, a little reminder of the finitude of earthly life." She also said that this illness could be a blessing for me, for it can be the impetus to decide how I want to spend the rest of my life.

A tap on the shoulder can take many forms, both positive and negative: illness, recovery from an illness, falling in love, the ending of a relationship, the loss of a job, the birth of a baby, the death of a loved one, a serious accident. Each tap asks us the question: "What do you want to do with the rest of your life?"

Loving God, may I be more sensitive to taps on the shoulder so I can decide how I want to spend the rest of my life.

WINTER

"Grace groweth best in winter."

SAMUEL RUTHERFORD

51. *The Lesson of the Afghan*

It is 5:30 AM and here I am sitting in the living room chair in my p.j.'s and robe, praying. Suddenly I feel chilly. So I reach for the afghan and drape it over my lap, legs, and slippered feet. Instantly I feel the warmth—as if the afghan were an electric blanket.

But, I remind myself, all the warmth I am feeling is *from me*. It is *my body* that is generating the heat. The afghan is merely "trapping" my heat and turning it back upon me, thus preventing my body's heat from dissipating into the chilly room. This trick of conserving self-generated heat has been employed by human beings for centuries in order to be comfortable and even to stay alive. In my mind's eye, I see people huddled together in a cave, or curled up under a piece of animal hide, or sleeping beneath a blanket woven from pliant grasses or sheep's wool. This morning, curled up under my afghan, I feel I am one with them.

There's a lesson here. Simply stated, it is this: I have many gifts and abilities—one of which is to generate heat. I must take advantage of my gifts and abilities to help myself, to nourish and sustain my own life. I must make use of my inherent God-given powers so they don't go to waste.

Jesus commanded us to love others—even our enemies. But love of others is rooted in a healthy love and appreciation for ourselves. And the more we love and appreciate ourselves, the freer we are to reach out to others selflessly. Today we might ask ourselves: What are some of my talents and abilities? How can they help nourish and sustain me? How can they help nourish and sustain others?

Source of all warmth, give me a greater awareness of my personal gifts today.

52. The Christmas Mug

A priest friend of mine went to a large discount store to buy a new Nativity set. When he didn't see any amid the Christmas items, he asked a clerk if they had any. "Oh, no," she said. "We don't sell stuff like that—only Christmas things."

"Only Christmas things." It amazes me how far removed our contemporary culture is from the real meaning of Christmas. Unfortunately, Christmas for the so-called secular world has been reduced to consumerism, that is, to sell, sell, sell and buy, buy, buy. The real meaning of Christmas—Jesus' birth into our world—is forgotten.

We have several Christmas mugs in our house. I dutifully bring them out each Christmas and pack them away afterward. But I've decided to keep one Christmas mug in use all year long. It is a green mug that says in bright red letters: "Jesus is the reason for the season." Why restrict its use to only the Christmas season? After all, Jesus is the reason for *every* season.

Jesus, may I never forget the true meaning of Christmas: your birth into our world.

53. *Survival*

Today as I was pulling out of our driveway, I spotted something moving on the road in front of me. At first I thought it was a leaf being blown across the road. But as I looked more closely, I saw it was a tiny mouse scurrying across the street.

I held my breath, for there were cars on that street and I was afraid one of them might hit him. But I sighed with relief when I saw the little creature safely reach the other side and disappear into the high grass. I wanted to call out to him, "Hey, Mr. Mouse. What is your goal for today?" I think I know (judging by how fast he was scurrying). He would have said: "Survival!"

I watched a television program about a pair of ostriches with their brood of six chicks. The program followed them for twenty-four hours. The poor ostrich parents were constantly on the alert for predators and other dangers. In the course of the day, they had to run away from a mongoose, chase away a warthog, and lead their young to edible grass. As the sun was setting, the announcer said something like this: "And so ends another day in the life of an ostrich. For this particular family, this day was a good one. A very good one. For all eight of them survived."

We humans expect much more from life than mere survival. We expect relaxation, pleasure, companionship, knowledge, success, peace, security, happiness. But we all know, there are some days when we are one with Mr. Mouse and the Ostrich Family: We count as a blessing the mere fact that we have survived another day. And we hope that tomorrow or the next day will give us something to survive for!

*When times are rough, God, may I count it a
blessing that, with your help, I have survived
another day.*

54. *Old Aunts and Old Houses*

My nephew John and his family live in an old Victorian house in
a small town in upper New York state. Over the past few years,
they have put a fair amount of labor and money into their house.
Recently John e-mailed me a picture of their house taken in 1896,
when the house was two years old. I wrote back to him saying,
"It's a great picture! The house was gorgeous—even in its youth."
Then I added, "But I think the house is even more beautiful today
than back then, for houses (like aunts) only get better with age!"

Imagine my surprise when John replied with this extended
metaphor:

"Yes, houses and aunts are alike in many ways. As they age
they develop idiosyncrasies in their character, requiring increas-
ing amounts of vigilant maintenance. They sometimes creak
and moan with the stress of age, settling a bit off-kilter, to the
point where their stability may come into question.

"It is imperative that these small nuisances not be neglected
so as to become severe structural problems requiring the attention of highly trained professionals. Left alone, they would
completely fall apart, becoming shadows of their former selves,
leaving us only to reminisce of their glory days gone by. Yes, it is
vital to nurture them along, accepting their foibles as inevitable
changes with age, treating them with the loving care they both
deserve and require."

God of youth, old age, and all the years in between, give me a tender affection for all the "old things" in my life.

55. *The Concordance to the Bible*

Sometimes I use a concordance to the Bible when I write. This is a thin volume that lists thousands of key words from the Bible and then gives the Scripture references where these words can be found. If I'm writing an article about angels, for example, I just look up the word "angel" in my concordance and find about a hundred references. If I want to see how many times the word "dog" is found in the Bible, I look it up in the concordance and note there are twenty-four occurrences. (There are none for "cat," by the way, but four for "caterpillar" and twenty-one for "cattle"!)

The other day I was leafing through the concordance to see which words have the most references. I was in the Ss. Which key words beginning with "S" do you think are found most frequently in the Bible? Take a minute to think.

If you said "sin," "spirit," or "son," you are on the right track, for each of those words has a multitude of references. But there are other words beginning with "S" with many Scripture references that you might not have thought of: "save," "see," "seek," and "servant." If these words are found so often in the Bible, they must be significant for our faith. We might ask ourselves: What significance do these four words have for my faith?

Jesus, continue to save me. Help me to see and seek you everywhere. May I become more and more of a servant for others as you were.

56. *Dispossession*

I was reading an article by Rowan Williams, head of the Anglican Church, where he said that the heart of mission is "dispossession," that is, the giving of ourselves away to others—as Jesus did. I happened to read that article at the time we had just moved my mother into a nursing home and were in the process of selling her house. I couldn't help but think, "Dispossession—that's what Mom's doing right now in a stark and painful way."

When my mother realized she could never live alone again, she began to divest herself of all her earthly possessions: her furniture, dishes, jewelry, knickknacks, linens—everything. My mother wanted to be fair, though, so she asked everyone—children and grandchildren—to write down four things of hers that they would like to have. We included a list of the major items. When the family members sent back their requests, Mom, my sister, and I went over the lists, making sure everyone got something nice they really wanted.

One by one the items were distributed: the maple dining room table and chairs, the new couch, the end tables, the antique oil lamps, the old coffee grinder, the cut glass vases and bowls from the Czech Republic. Some of the most prized possessions were those not worth much monetarily, but priceless in another way: my mother's cookbook, rolling pin, cookie jar, and the yellow ceramic duck and five ducklings that had graced her lawn for fifty years.

Mom dispossessed herself of these items by saying simply, "It's time. I won't be needing those things anymore." At the same time, she admitted to me one day that this was hard to do. "It's sad," she said, but she was consoled by the fact that many of her possessions would be staying in the family.

I believe my mother could divest herself of her possessions with such grace because she had spent her whole life giving herself away to others—to my father, us kids, the grandkids, and the great-grandkids. She gave herself away also to her friends, her parish, her work at the hospital, and numerous charities and good causes. In the end, this final dispossession of everything she owned was merely a continuation of all the previous ways she had given herself away to others her entire life.

How am I divesting myself of something at this particular time in my life?

Jesus, help me to give myself away to others just as you did.

57. *St. Paul*

St. Paul was zealous for the Gospel. He was gung ho for Jesus. Throughout his letters, he says some pretty wild things. For example, he calls himself "a fool for Christ" (1 Cor 4:10). In the letter to the Ephesians, he says he is "a prisoner of Christ Jesus" (3:1). He goes on to describe the incredible consequences of his relationship with Jesus: "We are weak…we go hungry and thirsty, we are poorly clad and roughly treated, we wander about homeless and we toil, working with our own hands" (1 Cor 4:10–12). Then he adds, "We have become the world's rubbish, the scum of all" (1 Cor 4:13). He describes his astonishing behavior as a disciple of Jesus: "When ridiculed, we bless; when persecuted, we endure; when slandered, we respond gently" (1 Cor 4:12–13).

Paul was totally one with Jesus. To one congregation he writes, "I have indeed been taken possession of by Christ Jesus" (Phil 3:12). To another he says, "I have been crucified with Christ; yet I live, no longer I, but Christ lives in me" (Gal 2:19–20). Because of this intense and intimate relationship with Jesus, Paul fears neither pain nor death. He says in one letter, "Now I rejoice in my sufferings for your sake" (Col 1:24). And in another, "For to me life is Christ, and death is gain" (Phil 1:21).

When I read Paul's passionate letters, I am tempted to say to him, "Cool your jets, Paul!" Or "Aren't you getting a little carried away?" Or "You're exaggerating, aren't you?"

Which only shows how bland and anemic my discipleship is.

Jesus, give me some of St. Paul's zeal and passion.

58. *Compassion*

In the 1992 Los Angeles riots, Bobby Green was the black man who came to the aid of Reginald Denny, the white truck driver who was being beaten. When asked why he risked his life to stop the beating, Green said simply, "It felt like *I* was getting hurt."

As the writer Frederick Buechner says, "Compassion is the sometimes fatal capacity for feeling what it is like inside somebody else's skin."

An important question to ask regularly is this: What sights arouse my compassion? A man being beaten up? A baby dying of malnutrition? An elderly woman sitting in a wheelchair in a nursing home corridor? A young soldier with no legs? A family of five living in a tent in a refugee camp? A loved one dying of cancer? But a far more important question is this: What do I *do* with my aroused compassion? Compassion alone won't save the world. But a compassionate *response* may help.

> *Compassionate Jesus, may my compassion move me to do good deeds for others.*

59. *Inklings*

The ultimate aim of the spiritual life is to let God win.

Our world is aglow with many burning bushes. But sometimes we fail to notice them. Or if we do spot them, we panic and grab the nearest fire extinguisher.

If we love only when it's convenient, we fall far short of Jesus' command. Calvary was not convenient.

There's a big difference between love and law. Love knows no limits, whereas law ordinarily delineates them. Love tells us to go the extra mile, whereas law says you can stop after 5,280 feet.

Telling the truth is not the same as speaking the truth. We tell the truth when we preach from pulpits. That's important and necessary. But we speak the truth when we pull up a chair next to someone in pain, listen to them, take their hand, and speak to them from our hearts and our own personal experience.

God of subtle movements, give clarity to all my inklings.

60. *Poor Me*

Sometimes we use the words "poor me" as an excuse for not living Jesus' teachings.

Poor me, we say, I'm so old...so young...so middle-aged.

Poor me, I'm so ordinary...so deprived...so deficient.

Poor me, I'm so weak...so tired...so inferior.

Poor me, I'm a sinner.

But Poor Me is not an excuse for inaction.

In fact, it lies at the very core of my discipleship.

Poor Me is the very reason I need a Savior in the first place!

So say not: Poor me!

Say instead:

Poor me—I need Jesus!

Lucky me, I've got him!

Jesus, help me to realize how lucky I am to have you as savior and friend.

61. *"I Am with You Always"*

Jesus made this promise to his disciples: "And behold, I am with you always, to the end of the age" (Mt 28:20). It is a promise made to all of his followers down through the ages—including us, including me. He says, "I am with you always." Notice, he sets no qualifications. He doesn't say I am with you when you're good…when you're successful…when you have clarity of vision…when you feel my presence. No, he says simply, "I am with you always"—no matter what.

This steadfast presence of Jesus in our personal life, in our church, and in our world is immensely comforting for me. No matter what our circumstances, Jesus is with us. How encouraging! But it is also extremely challenging. For Jesus is present not only to comfort and encourage, but also to nudge, prod, and press us to reach out to those who are in need in any way. His presence goads us into living our life unselfishly in line with his example and teachings.

Jesus is here. What is he urging me to do today?

Jesus, I count on your presence in my life. Keep urging me to love others.

62. *Dressing Room Mirrors*

The older I get, the less eager I am to try on clothes in those dressing rooms provided by clothing stores. My reluctance comes from several factors.

First, trying on clothes is an ordeal for me. It wears me out. Second, buying new clothes just doesn't carry the excitement it did when I was younger. And third, I don't particularly like the thought of seeing my nearly naked body reflected back to me in all those mirrors.

As if one mirror weren't enough, some dressing rooms have mirrors on three sides. They also have bright lights that illuminate every part of your figure. So there's no escaping what your body looks like—unless you undress with your eyes closed. If you're young and/or have an attractive figure, you probably have no idea why these dressing rooms upset me. The rest of you, who are like me—with substantial mileage on your frame and/or some extra pounds—know what I'm talking about. When I see myself in the mirrors, I am sometimes shocked. I find myself asking questions like these: "When did I get that big stomach?...How come the skin on my upper arms is sagging like that? It never used to!...I once had perfect posture. When did I get stooped?"

When I share my feelings about dressing rooms with women friends, I learn I am not alone. It seems everyone has her dressing room horror story to tell. We listen to each other's tales, we console one another, and we usually end up laughing about the whole thing. There seems to be camaraderie even in this minor misery of life. Thank God!

God, you know me completely—inside and out— and yet you still love me. Help me to accept my imperfections and the imperfections of others.

63. *The Miracle of Being*

In her book *Making the Shift: Seeing Faith through a New Lens*, Elaine Prevallet, SL, says, "It is not uncommon for me, often without trying, to experience the miracle of being." She goes on to explain: "I mean the miracle of my own being and the miracle of everything that is. I mean the miracle that there is *anything* rather than *nothing*."

That I am, that I am I, is a miracle. That you exist, that you are you, is also a miracle. That a peacock spreads its gorgeous tail, that a cat has thirty muscles in each ear, that the Grand Canyon is more than two billion years old—all, all are miracles. Prevallet raises the question, "Why is there anything at all, let alone this whole magnificent universe?"

Good question.

We are quick to thank God for particular things: our family, our eyesight, the sunrise, blueberries. And that's good. But maybe we don't thank God enough just for existence.

Creator God, I thank you that I am, and that I am I.

64. *The Christmas "Giving Tree"*

Every Advent, our parish has a "Giving Tree" in the gathering space of our church. On the branches are hung hundreds of paper tags shaped like stars or Christmas tree ornaments. On each tag is the first name, age, size, and Christmas wish of someone in need. I am always amazed that every Advent, all the tags are taken by our parishioners.

I like to take a tag, too. I enjoy buying a specific gift for a specific person. I confess though, I used to peek at the tags and take the name of a child. I liked buying a toy for a child and throwing in some clothes and maybe a book.

But lately I've been purposely taking the name of an adult. One year I had a man, fifty-six, who asked simply for a T-shirt. I got him five. They were on sale. Another time I had a fifty-year-old woman who wanted a nightgown. She got a nightgown, some body lotion, and a gift certificate to a local store.

I wrap the gifts carefully, realizing (sadly) that my gift may be the only one this person gets for Christmas.

I always pray for the individuals and their families, too. I also pray for the people who supply us with the names and who ultimately distribute the gifts. The Advent "Giving Tree" in our parish is one way love is made visible each year.

Incarnate God, expand our hearts at Christmas and all year round.

65. *The God of Many Chances*

The Book of Jonah tells the story of the conversion of the great city of Nineveh through the preaching of the prophet Jonah. So thorough was the conversion that even the cattle and sheep got into the act of massive repentance. But one of my favorite lines from the story is this one: "The word of the Lord came to Jonah *a second time.*"

We all remember what happened the first time the word of the Lord came to Jonah. He ran away from God. It took a stopover in the belly of a whale to convince Jonah to do what God had asked him to do.

It took two tries for Jonah to get it right. I find that consoling. Sometimes it takes me two tries—or ten or even a hundred tries—to get something right. Just when I think I have finally mastered patience, for example, I become upset at something trivial. Just when I respond generously to another's need, I find myself pulling back from a new request for help. Just when I begin to trust God completely, I find myself beginning to doubt God's love and care for me.

Rabbi Harold Kushner has said, "The challenge of being human is so great, no one gets it right every time." Thank God our God is a God of many chances!

Loving God, thank you for the many chances you give me to get life right.

66. *We Are Sojourners*

In the first letter of St. Peter, we are told we are sojourners in a foreign land. We are pilgrims in a place that is not our home. I don't know about you, but there are times I feel very much at home on Planet Earth, thank you. I feel I am a real resident of this earthly life, something of a permanent fixture. I have family, friends, a nice house to live in, plenty of food, a pleasant neighborhood, and a country that ensures certain basic human rights and offers many opportunities. Why would I not feel at home here?

Yet, there are times when I am confronted by the temporariness of my life here on earth. Perhaps I get a bad report from my doctor, lose a loved one, experience a financial crisis, undergo a major setback, or just feel unfulfilled and restless. At such times, the words of Scripture strike home: Earth is not my final destination. I'm only passing through.

This realization affects the way I live, the choices I make, the way I relate to others. Above all, it keeps me moving forward. It prevents me from getting too attached to "worldly things." It encourages me to form relationships with other sojourners who are traveling the same road. It encourages me to keep going even when I experience my innate restlessness, disappointments, and the ultimate inadequacy of all things.

Someone once said life here on earth is not the full symphony. That's right. It's merely the first movement. The full symphony is yet to come.

Loving God, I am a sojourner on earth. Help me to keep moving forward toward you.

67. *I Don't Want to Live in This World Any Longer*

It was a small article on page nine in yesterday's newspaper. Somewhere in Afghanistan, a group of about twelve children were walking along a city street on their way home from school. A security camera caught them, the article said—their laughter, their pausing to shift their books. In the background, a car can be seen coming slowly down the street, weaving between the barricades put up for security purposes. As the car gets beside the children, there is a massive explosion. In an instant the children are engulfed in flames. All of them are killed by a suicide bomber.

I can't stop thinking about those children and the terrible, heinous act that took their young lives. All day long I can't get them off my mind. I think about their parents, too—their agony, grief, and anger. I find myself saying to God, "God, I don't want to live in this world any longer. I can't bear to stay in a world where little children are blown up—intentionally. Take me from this awful place. I don't care where you put me. Hell can't be any worse than this."

Later, I try to tell myself that this bombing was an isolated act by a few deranged individuals. I tell myself that this world is filled with good people who love and care for children every single day—parents, grandparents, teachers, health care personnel, social workers. But right now, that does little to ease my pain. These specific children are dead. Killed intentionally in an awful way by other human beings. For now, my heart will not be consoled.

Loving God, what small steps can I take to put more love into a world that desperately needs it?

68. *St. Joseph*

Scripture does not quote a single word by St. Joseph. That doesn't mean he never said anything. But it does mean what Joseph *did* far outweighed anything he could have *said*.

What did Joseph do? He did the kinds of things we all do. For example, he related to other people. He no doubt interacted with his family, friends, and his fellow townspeople. When we first meet Joseph in Scripture, he is engaged to Mary.

But Joseph also suffered distress—as we do, too. When he learned his fiancée was pregnant, he was so upset he couldn't sleep. But in his distress, Joseph sought direction from God. When, through an angel at night, God told Joseph to take Mary as his wife and raise the child as his own, Joseph did as he was directed. Later, when that same angel warned him of Herod's wicked plans, Joseph fled with his family into a foreign land.

And finally, the gospels tell us, Joseph worked. And like most of us, his work wasn't glamorous or showy. He was a simple carpenter, toiling hard every day to support his family.

In a culture that bombards us with words, we need a saint like Joseph to remind us that, when it comes to our faith, what we *do* is far more important than what we *say*. And listening to the angels God sends into our life is far more crucial than gabbing all day long.

Saint Joseph, help me to imitate your faith, your listening, and your obedience to God's word.

69. *Let Real Life Begin—Again*

The writer Alfred D. Souza said: "For a long time it had seemed to me that life was about to begin—real life. But there was always some obstacle in the way, something to be gotten through first, some unfinished business, time still to be served, a debt to be paid. Then life would begin. At last it dawned on me that these obstacles were my life."

There is always the temptation to think of real life as something in the future—after I get my own apartment, after I earn my degree, after I marry, after I get that promotion, after the kids finish college, after I become more mature, after I learn to pray. Little wonder that one of the cherished practices of traditional spirituality is living in the present moment. For that's where real life is. That's where God is. The things I see as obstacles to real living are what real living is all about.

Every morning, we might want to pray these words: "Let real life begin again for me today."

God of all time, give me a greater appreciation of living in the present moment.

70. *Quotations on Adversity*

"An inconvenience is only an adventure wrongly considered; and adventure is an inconvenience rightly considered."
• *G.K. Chesterton*

"The fullness of life is in the hazards of life." • *Edith Hamilton*

Old Midwestern adage: "Son, you don't have a problem. You've got a decision to make."

"The lowest ebb is the turn of the tide." • *Henry W. Longfellow*

"Problems are only opportunities in work clothes."
• *Henry J. Kaiser*

"The art of living is more like wrestling than dancing."
• *Marcus Aurelius*

God of my whole life, help me to face my adversities with patience and trust.

71. *On Beauty and Becoming Human*

Someone has said that, in one sense, we are not *born* human. We *become* human by the experiences we undergo and the choices we make. This same person said that one of the major factors that contributes to our humanness is the experience of beauty.

We must make time for beauty in our lives—in whatever form we prefer. Some of us are quick to find beauty in the natural world. We frequent parks, we fuss over our gardens, we pay attention to birds, we adorn our homes with flowers, we take note of the changes in the seasons outside our kitchen windows. Some of us find beauty in literature. We read good books, we memorize lines from immortal poems, we are drawn to thought-provoking plays and movies. Still others find beauty in the visual arts. We regularly go to art museums and can get lost in a room filled with Impressionist paintings, Indian pottery, or contemporary photography.

The writer D.H. Lawrence said it well when he wrote: "The human soul needs beauty even more than it needs bread."

Source of all beauty, feed me with beauty today.

72. *Winter: The Misunderstood Season*

I recently came across a web page devoted to winter. The author calls winter "the most misunderstood season of all." He addresses his words to those people (like me) who live in places where winter is characterized by ice, snow, and freezing temperatures. And throughout his page, he reminds us of some of the beauties of this season.

He says, for example, that winter is "a beautiful season of intimacy and reflection (that) gives us the opportunity to stay inside and look inside." He quotes individuals like the artist Andrew Wyeth who said, "I prefer winter and fall, when you feel the bone structure of the landscape—the loneliness of it, the dead feeling of winter. Something waits beneath it, the whole story doesn't show."

Personally I am often mesmerized by the falling snow. I like what Adrienne Ivey wrote about the snow: "Everything is equal in the snow: all trees, all lawns, all streets, all rooftops, all cars. Everything is white, white, white, as far as you can see." The manicured lawns and the neglected lawns look the same after a snowfall. So do the just-bought car and the old jalopy. "Everything looks clean and fresh and unmarred by time or use. Snow…is a great leveler."

I also appreciate the quiet of a winter landscape. Snow muffles all sounds. Because of the absence of colors in winter, you appreciate color even more when it chances by. Is there anything more breathless to behold in winter than a bright red cardinal flitting among the snow-covered branches of a tree?

I suppose the real gift is to appreciate all the seasons—the seasons of the natural world as well as the seasons of the heart.

*Creator of all seasons, give me the gift to
find beauty and goodness in all the seasons
of my life.*

73. *Jigsaw Puzzles*

I enjoy putting jigsaw puzzles together—especially during the
winter months and preferably with one or two other people. I've
reflected on why I like jigsaw puzzles so much, and I've come up
with the following reasons:

1. There is a solution to a jigsaw puzzle (unlike some of the
other puzzles in my life).

2. There are a few tricks you can learn to make it easier to put
a puzzle together. Start with the frame, for example. Sort the
pieces according to color or shape. Refer to the picture on the
box—unless, of course, you think that's cheating.

3. When doing a puzzle, you see progress no matter how tough
the puzzle may be. In real life, you don't always see progress for
the work you do.

4. Every piece of the puzzle is important. If one piece is missing,
the puzzle isn't whole. This fact reminds me of the importance
of every aspect of my life and every human being. All the pieces
make a vital contribution to the whole picture.

5. Doing jigsaw puzzles trains your powers of observation and
differentiation. At first, all the blues may look alike, for instance,
but as you study them more closely you begin to notice subtle
differences in the shades of blue. Many times you eventually

differentiate between four or five different blues that had previously looked all the same. Hopefully, this honing of the powers of observation and differentiation will carry over into other aspects of our lives.

6. Puzzles teach us patience. Enough said.

7. Puzzles are somewhat addictive. How? By rewarding us for our labors. Many times I have stood up and been tempted to walk away from a puzzle because I haven't found a piece for quite some time. But suddenly I find a piece that fits, I put it in, and then I sit down again, hooked into putting in "just one more piece."

8. There's great satisfaction when you put the final piece in the puzzle. As I press it in, I usually celebrate it with a "Ta da!" or a clap of my hands. If several of us have labored over the puzzle for quite a while, we celebrate with high fives all around.

God of the whole picture, help me to be patient with solving the puzzles of my life, entrusting their final solution to you.

74. *Heroes of Social Justice*

In her book *Guests of God*, Monika Hellwig points to certain strides made worldwide over the years to improve social conditions, especially for those who are poor: child labor laws, free public schooling, bankruptcy laws, public welfare, legislation on factory conditions, minimum wage requirements, civil rights laws, and much more. She adds, "But such developments take time. They seldom happened in the lifetimes of those who first took the initiative to respond."

Many of the people we honor as heroes of charity or social justice simply did privately what they could about the suffering and injustice they saw before their own eyes. John Bosco rounded up neglected working-class boys in Turin, Italy, and began to teach them. Harriet Tubman personally led more than 300 slaves to freedom in the North. In Budapest, Hungary, Raoul Wallenberg used clever diplomatic tactics to save thousands of Jews from Nazi death camps. Dorothy Day opened a soup kitchen and shelter for the homeless of New York City. Rosa Parks defied racial segregation on a bus in Montgomery, Alabama, and was subsequently arrested.

Today we, too, have many opportunities to respond to injustices in whatever form we see them. But militating against our involvement is the temptation to think we are "only one" and that the systemic changes still needed are far beyond our own power. Maybe so. But are we willing to invest time and effort in a cherished cause whose success we may not live to see?

God of justice and mercy, inspire me to do one small act today about an injustice I see before my eyes.

75. At Home with Death

For six years, I served as provincial for my religious community. During that time we buried sixty-one of our sisters. Sixty-one! That meant I prayed at their death beds, attended every wake, and wrote and delivered the eulogy at every funeral. Most of these sisters I knew well. Some had been my teachers. Others I had lived and worked with. Most were in their seventies, eighties, and nineties when they died. One was only fifty-one. Some died after a prolonged illness. A few died suddenly and unexpectedly.

During those same six years, I also buried my father, three aunts, and an uncle. In addition, I attended the wakes and funerals of dozens of other people, most notably the parents and siblings of the sisters. I suppose you can say that during those six years, I was somewhat "at home with death," that is, I was never far removed from the stark and mysterious reality of death.

Looking back, I now see how all these deaths helped me (paradoxically) to live a better life. They made me more appreciative of the preciousness of each individual. They heightened my awareness of the value of time—each year, each day, each moment.

The many deaths provided me with a context in which to make daily decisions, a backdrop against which to sort my priorities. Witnessing so many deaths also helped me to be less fearful of my own death. I began to see death more and more as a natural part of the living process, just another step in our life's journey.

The many deaths also constantly challenged my faith. They forced me to ponder and pray about my belief in Jesus' Resurrection and what that "article of faith" means to me personally. The deaths also raised many questions for me about eternity and the great final reunion with all of my loved ones.

In her book *Bird by Bird*, Anne Lamott writes, "My deepest belief is that to live as if we're dying can set us free. Dying people teach you to pay attention and to forgive and not to sweat the small stuff."

What do dying people teach me?

God of life and death, may the remembrance of my own mortality make me a more attentive, forgiving, and patient person.

SPRING

"The day the Lord created hope was probably the same day he created spring."

BERN WILLIAMS

76. *Quotations on Spring*

"If spring came but once a century, instead of once a year, or burst forth with the sound of an earthquake, and not in silence, what wonder and expectation there would be in all hearts to behold the miraculous change!" ◆ *Henry W. Longfellow*

"The world's favorite season is the spring. All things seem possible in May." ◆ *Edwin Way Teale*

"The peace and beauty of a spring day has descended upon the earth like a benediction." ◆ *Kate Chopin*

"Science has never drummed up quite as effective a tranquilizing agent as a sunny spring day." ◆ *W. Earl Hall*

"All through the long winter, I dream of my garden. On the first day of spring, I dig my fingers into the soft earth. I can feel its energy, and my spirits soar." ◆ *Helen Hayes*

"Everything is blooming most recklessly; if it were voices instead of colors, there would be an unbelievable shrieking into the heart of the night." ◆ *Rainer Maria Rilke*

"Spring is when you feel like whistling even with a shoe full of slush." ◆ *Doug Larson*

"Spring is God's way of saying, 'One more time!'"
  ◆ *Robert Orben*

Creator of all seasons, I thank you for spring.

77. *Did Jesus Dance?*

Did Jesus dance? We don't know for sure, but chances are he did. In Jesus' time, dancing was customary at weddings, for example, although men danced in a group with other men, and women with other women. So besides working his first miracle at the wedding feast in Cana, Jesus probably also danced there.

The thought of Jesus' turning the water into wine gladdens my heart. After all, I like wine. And I also like the fact that Jesus worked his first miracle at the request of his mother for the sole purpose (it seems) of preserving a young couple from embarrassment—and to prolong the celebration.

But the thought of Jesus dancing—now that's something that really delights me. I picture him stamping his feet, clapping his hands over his head, swaying, laughing, and turning around. Maybe he even sang the words of some of the songs that were played. What an image! Has anyone ever drawn a picture of a dancing Jesus?

It was the German philosopher Friedrich Nietzsche who said, "I could believe only in a God who knows how to dance." Me too. And in Jesus, God did dance.

Jesus, when life becomes burdensome for me, invite me to dance.

78. My To-Do List

I'm always making to-do lists. On a little piece of paper I jot down all the jobs I have to do: pick up prescription, call Kathy, send handouts to Tom, print boarding pass, wash clothes, return library books, get eggs, work on poetry book. I write these tasks down so I don't forget to do them. I also write them down, because I get a keen sense of satisfaction every time I cross something off my list. I've even been known to do this crazy thing: If I accomplish a task I forgot to write on my list, I write it down anyway and then cross it off! I suspect I am not the only person in the world who does this silly thing!

In her book *Seven Sacred Pauses*, Macrina Wiederkehr, OSB, writes about living more "mindfully," that is, living more attentively in the present moment. One way to facilitate this "mindful living" is by pausing intentionally throughout the day to be more aware of the world around us and inside us. When we do this, says Wiederkehr, "Suddenly we see the aura of holy light exuding from all things." She adds, "It will be a happy moment when we remember to add the wise act of *pausing* to our to-do lists."

Her words made me wonder: What other "tasks" might we add that we seldom put on our to-do lists? Perhaps "tasks" such as these: smell the coffee, hum, thank God for something you seldom thank God for, notice people's eyes, breathe slowly and deeply for three minutes, talk to a plant, contemplate your hands, listen to some silence, name three things that are right in your life right now.

God of my entire life, help me to live more mindful of "the aura of holy light exuding from all things."

79. Wondering about Death at a Baseball Game

Sometimes when I'm in a large crowd—like sitting in the stadium at a Cleveland Indians game—I'm tempted to stand up and shout to everyone within earshot, "Excuse me, people, but do you realize we're all going to die? That in a hundred years, chances are, not one of us sitting in this stadium here today is going to be alive!" And if the fans don't glare me into silence, boo me to shut up, or yell at me to "sit down, for crying out loud," I'd continue.

"Do any of you ever think about your own death? Huh? Do you? Well, I do! Not constantly, of course. That would be crazy. But I do think about it on a regular basis. I wonder about the when and how of my death. Will it be sudden or drawn out? Will I be alone or with other people? Will I die inside a building or outside? In a bed, in a wrecked car, or on some path in a park? And what exactly does death feel like anyway? Is there excruciating pain despite all our modern drugs? Or is it eventually painless? Will I go eagerly into that good night or will I hold back in terror? Will I see Jesus face to face? Will I see my loved ones who have already gone before me? And what in the heck does life after death feel like?"

By now several security guards will probably be escorting me out of the stadium. But I will add for everyone to hear, "I was just wondering, that's all."

God of the living and the dead, may the remembrance of my own death give meaning and direction to my life.

80. *God's Voice Mail*

Whenever I return from a trip, I listen to my voice mail. I usually find several messages: a friend inviting me out to lunch, a colleague reminding me of a meeting, a member of a certain parish asking me to give a talk, or my sister calling just to chat.

This makes me wonder: What kind of a message would *Jesus* leave on my voice mail? Perhaps he would say, "Hi, friend! I just called to see how you're doing." Or "Can we get together soon?" Or "I want to thank you for all you're doing for me." Or maybe his words would be the words he spoke to his disciples after the Resurrection, "Peace I leave with you; my peace I give to you" (Jn 14:27).

In one way, the daily Scripture readings are like God's voice mail to us. They are God's daily reminders of what's really important in life. They provide encouragement and direction. They inspire and also challenge. The people and events in our everyday lives can also be messages from God. They, too, can inform, advise, console, ask things of us, and point the way for us. Do we take time to listen to this divine voice mail? If we do, then how do we respond to the messages we receive?

Jesus, help me to listen to your messages in the Scripture, people, and events of this day.

81. *God Wants Me to Be* _____

Fill in the blank with one word:

God wants me to be _____.

Take your time. Think about it for a minute. What word did you put in the blank? Good? Happy? Loving? Obedient? Honest? Humble? Or did you put something else in the blank—like creative, funny, daring, extravagant, spunky?

What we think God wants us to be will guide our actions and choices. It will form the person we will become. Which word we put into the blank is of supreme importance. After all, there's a big difference between believing God wants us to be compassionate and believing God wants us to be hygienic.

God, what do you want me to be?

82. *The Annunciation*

Someone has said, "All of mystical theology is contained in the Annunciation." That may well be true.

Here's the pattern as I see it:

God invites.
We're allowed to be surprised,
confused, or even frightened.
We're also permitted to ask a question or two.
God may offer some clarification,
but it's usually nothing very specific.
No blueprints. No scripts or maps.
In the end, we must trust the Inviter.
That's all. That's *all*.

So we say our "yes" and "thy will be done."
Then we'd better hang on for dear life.
For when we say "yes" to God,
nothing in our dear life
will ever be the same again.
Ever.

*God who invites me daily, help me to say my "yes"
and "thy will be done" to you.*

83. *More Inklings*

Asceticism means being free enough to do willingly and cheerfully what is not our first preference.

Spite is dislike with nails attached.

God can use wee things to teach us humongous truths.

Sometimes laws fail to achieve one of law's ultimate purposes: to protect the weak from the strong. Why do they fail? Because the strong make most of the laws.

Friendship can start on its own. But it needs the attentiveness of both parties in order to grow, thrive, and endure.

Grant clarity to all my inklings, God.

84. *Blessed Un-assurance*

We are seldom given assurance that our mission in life is effective. Jesus had no such assurance. Neither did the saints. Why should it be any different for us?

Oh, yes, occasionally we sense that our good works are making a difference in the world. Perhaps someone smiles at us, says a shy "thank you" to us, or tells us we've been "so kind" or "very helpful." But such assurances are soon swallowed up in the darkness of indifference. And we trudge on, trying to put love where there is none or adding to love where it already exists. We do this not because we know that our loving is effective, but because we believe that loving is the most important thing we can do in the world.

The Czech writer and statesman Vaclav Havel has written: "Work for something because it is good, not just because it stands a chance to succeed."

Gracious God, help me to live with fewer assurances—except the assurance of your love for me.

85. *Necessary Burdens*

In the Acts of the Apostles, we read about a controversy in the early Church. It seems some of the Christians wanted Gentile converts to embrace Jewish religious practices (such as circumcision) when they became Christians. Others, including St. Paul, strongly opposed the idea, saying that God does not want to place unnecessary burdens on anyone. The latter group's opinion eventually prevailed.

Unnecessary burdens. The phrase implies that some burdens are necessary. They are part and parcel of our religious faith and our response to God's call. What might some of these burdens be? The fidelity to prayer, the daily struggle against selfishness, the commitment to social justice, the call to forgiveness, to name a few. But other burdens are unnecessary and arise out of fear, guilt, or mistrust in God's love for us. Such burdens might include compulsive prayers, scrupulosity, superstitious religious practices, debilitating worry.

A grace to pray for: to be freed from the burdens of our own making in order to bear generously the burdens of Christian loving.

Jesus, free me from unnecessary burdens and strengthen me to bear the necessary burdens of Christian love.

86. Notice What You Notice

One day Jesus and his disciples were standing outside the temple as people came by and made contributions to the temple treasury. Luke's gospel says this of Jesus: "...and he noticed a poor widow putting in two small coins" (21:2).

Two words stand out in that sentence for me: *he noticed.* They speak volumes about Jesus' sensitivity, perception, and priorities. Jesus doesn't focus on the obvious—those wealthy individuals who, in a showy manner, are depositing their large contributions into the treasury. No, he notices the poor widow as she quickly and unobtrusively tosses in her two tiny coins and scurries away. Not only does Jesus notice her, he appreciates the significance of what she has done: She who seemed to give the *least* has, in reality, given the *most*. Why? Because, as Jesus says, "she, from her poverty, has offered her whole livelihood" (Lk 21:4). In other words, she gave her all.

For the next few days, we might want to notice what we notice. Do we notice only the obvious, or are we sensitive to the subtle? Do we notice only what's wrong with the world, or do we also see what's right? Do we notice only people's shortcomings, or are we mindful of their good points? If we pay attention to our noticing, we may realize like Jesus that things are not always what they seem. Sometimes they're better.

Jesus, help me to notice and appreciate the subtle goodness within and around me.

87. *The Book of Jonah*

I get a kick out of the Book of Jonah. I like Jonah's unwillingness to do what God asks him to do: preach repentance to his enemies, the Ninevites. Jonah's unwillingness mirrors my own unwillingness to do God's bidding at times. I also like the fierce storm in the story, the uprightness of Jonah's shipmates, and his preference for death rather than seeing his enemies converted and forgiven by God.

Of course, I like the whale part, too. Like Jonah, I've been in some tight spots. I know what it means to sit curled up and brooding. Then there's the fresh "second chance" God gives to Jonah to get it right. Jonah does get it right the second time. He agrees to preach to the Ninevites—although he does so grudgingly.

Jonah delivers God's message of repentance. Despite his lack of enthusiasm, his words are met with the wholesale conversion of the entire wicked city (as writer Alice Camille puts it) "from the king down to the cows, dogs and parakeets." That's pretty inclusive!

God forgives the Ninevites, and Jonah goes to sit and pout under a *kikayon* bush, a wide-leafed plant of the cucumber family. (Don't you just love little details like that?) Jonah is angry that God has used his preaching to move so many hearts. But what he's really angry about, of course, is that God has forgiven the people he (Jonah) despises. He had hoped God would be more provincial with his love, more selective with his compassion. But no, Jonah learns that God's love and forgiveness spill over onto everyone. *Every one!* No wonder Jonah pouts. He thought he and his people had a monopoly on God's love.

There's even more to the story. God, by example, is really asking Jonah to love in the same way God loves—profusely, prodigally, lavishly. Jonah's love and forgiveness also must extend even to his archenemies. That's a tall order for Jonah. It's the same tall order given to us.

It's little wonder Jonah sits and pouts. And it's little wonder we do, too, at times.

God of extravagant love, help me to extend the borders of my love and forgiveness.

88. *The Need for Security*

How strong is my need for security? The first disciples, when they chose to follow Jesus, seemed to walk away from the security of their ordinary lives. Peter, Andrew, and the Zebedee brothers left their fishing nets and boats on the shore when they became Jesus' disciples. Matthew walked away from his money table and his job as a tax collector. James the Zealot disassociated himself from his radical "political party." Others severed themselves from their allegiance to John the Baptist.

In short, they were not held prisoner by their need for security. They were not stifled by the need to cling to their ordinary way of living. When they became disciples, they risked living in an entirely new way.

Does my need for security prevent me from taking risks for the Gospel? What nets am I willing to leave on the shore, what groups am I willing to forsake, what lake am I willing to turn my back to—if doing so is the cost I have to pay to follow Jesus?

Demanding Jesus, may my need for security never prevent me from following you more closely.

89. *Six Reasons to Be Hopeful*

Sometimes we need some concrete reasons to be hopeful. Here are a few facts that help me when I am feeling hopeless:

1. Wars and terrorism always make the headlines, but the fact is many of the world's 6.7 billion people now live in peace. In fact,

a person's chance of dying from war or violence today is less than two percent—much lower than earlier generations.

2. In 1970, barely half the people in the world were literate. Today, more than eighty percent of the world's people can read.

3. For centuries, slavery was a common practice. Even in countries such as the United States, this terrible injustice was supported and protected by law. Today slavery is outlawed in most countries in our world.

4. In many countries, children are more protected by laws than ever before in human history.

5. During the Cold War the United States and the Soviet Union had about 50,000 nuclear warheads between them. Since then, tens of thousands of those weapons have been eliminated. In his book *The Progress Paradox*, Gregg Easterbrook writes, "Historians will view nuclear arms reduction as such an incredible accomplishment that it will seem bizarre in retrospect so little attention was paid while it was happening."

6. Progress in medicine has virtually rid the world of diseases that once killed millions of people: smallpox, bubonic plague, typhoid, polio.

These signs of progress must not make us complacent. There is still much work to be done in all the areas listed above. At the same time, these signs can give us hope as we work to bring about a more just world.

> *God of Hope, I thank you for the progress we have made as a human family. Give us the grace to continue to work for a better world.*

90. *God's Greatest Stoop*

Sometimes I watch TV programs that try to help parents deal with their children. One point the so-called experts stress is for parents to stoop down to their children's level when talking to them—especially if they're correcting them or having a serious conversation with them. As adults, we easily forget how much bigger we are than our children. We usually tower over them, forgetting how much our size alone can intimidate them. One expert on raising children stood on a picnic table once and yelled down at a father—so he would feel what his children were experiencing when he stood over them and yelled down at them.

This emphasis on stooping down recalls these lines: "I waited, waited for the Lord; who bent down and heard my cry" (Ps 40:2). This image of God stooping down to my level to listen and to speak to me is a tender one. I find it immensely comforting.

God stoops down to me, to us. In fact, one way to view the incarnation is to think of it as God's Greatest Stoop. The infinite, almighty God took on a lowly human body and entered our small world. In the person of Jesus, God became one of us, taking upon himself our perspective, our limitations, our vulnerability. How much God loves us, the children of God!

Loving God who stoops down to me, give me the grace to be tender and patient with everyone I meet today—especially children.

91. *The 300-Year-Old Oak Tree*

I made a trip today to the huge oak tree in our woods. It was more pilgrimage than trip, for I went with a religious purpose: to pay homage to the tree. I longed to see, touch, and be with a life form that is estimated to be more than 300 years old. As I neared the tree, it didn't seem as big as I remembered it from the last time I visited. But from a distance, looks can be deceiving. As I got closer to the tree, its massive size became very apparent. Its trunk is so wide it takes about six people with outstretched arms to encircle it. Its branches are so high I couldn't see the top of the tree no matter what angle I tried. In its presence, I was compelled to bow respectfully before it. I was even tempted to take off my sneakers as a sign of reverence, but the ground was too cold and muddy. How does one properly venerate something—someone—so old?

I did go up to it and fingered its trunk with my hands. The bark was hard and ridged. I put the palms of my hands on its trunk and closed my eyes, hoping to connect with the life force inside this ancient tree. Then I hugged it—as best I could considering its huge circumference. And then I thanked the old oak tree *for being*—for being so old, for being so beautiful.

I began to imagine all the storms this tree had experienced in its lifetime. Does it remember the huge snowstorm of 1952? The tornado of 1968? The massive blizzard of 1978? Those storms were all part of my lifetime. But perhaps there were far worse storms in the 1800s or 1700s. If this tree could talk, maybe it would say, "You should have seen the blizzard of 1734 or the tornado of 1815! Now those were really storms!"

And what about the droughts? How many of those did this oak weather over 300 years? I noticed the tree stands beside a creek that has very little water in it now, but who knows how deep and wide that creek might have been over the past 300 years? And what about diseases and insect infestations? And what about other trees that encroached upon its space when it was young? How did it survive all the vicissitudes of life?

So many questions. So much mystery. After a few more moments of prayer, I slowly walked away, filled with wonder and respect for one old oak that has stood its ground for three centuries.

Eternal God, I thank you for all things old and enduring.

92. *Quotations on Love*

"Unless you love someone, nothing makes sense."

◆ *W.H. Auden*

"The love of neighbor in all its fullness simply means being able to say to him: 'What are you going through?'" ◆ *Simone Weil*

"Almsgiving is the mother of love." ◆ *St. John Chrysostom*

Father Zosima in *The Brothers Karamazov* by Fyodor Dostoyevsky: "Love in practice is a hard and dreadful thing compared to love in dreams."

"Love is the only force capable of transforming an enemy into a friend." ◆ *Martin Luther King Jr.*

"To love another person is to see the face of God."

◆ Les Misérables *by Victor Hugo*

"To love another person is to *be* the face of God."

◦ *Patricia Livingston*

Source of all love, help me to love like you.

93. *Plan B*

When I ask friends out for a meal, I usually ask them to mark down two dates. That way, if something unexpected comes up, preventing us from meeting on the first date, we already have a backup date penciled on our calendars. I learned long ago that when making plans, it's always good to have a Plan B, just in case something makes Plan A impossible.

I have never kept track of how many times I have had to resort to Plan B, but it is fairly often. My plans don't always go as I want them to go—in both small ways and big ways. I plan on getting to the important meeting on time, but I get a flat tire instead. I go in for what I plan to be a routine physical, only to get a serious diagnosis from my doctor. As John Lennon remarked, "If you want to make God laugh, just tell God your plans."

That's not to say we shouldn't make plans, of course. After all, planning is one way we channel our time, energy and talents into activities that are necessary, worthwhile, and helpful to others. We plan many things—our work, meetings, meals, household chores, errands, parties, liturgical celebrations, vacations. But when we make plans, we must not be wedded to them to such an extent that we are totally discombobulated when things do not go our way.

Scripture is filled with individuals whom God asked to change their plans in a major way. In doing so, they were the better for it—and we're the better for it, too. Abraham and Sarah, for example, were an elderly couple who were probably planning their retirement in their homeland of Ur. But God changed their plans, asking them to uproot themselves from their familiar world and travel to a land they had never even heard of before. Moses planned to make his living as a shepherd for his father-in-law, but God changed his plans by calling him to leave those flocks and to lead the Israelites out of the slavery of Egypt. Mary planned to marry Joseph and raise an ordinary family in an ordinary way in an ordinary town. But God asked her to radically alter her plans and become the mother of the Messiah.

How stubbornly do we hang on to our plans? In what ways has life turned out for us as we planned—and as we didn't plan? Has a change of our plans ever made us the better for it?

God, give me the grace to graciously change my plans whenever you ask it of me.

94. *Easter*

For many of us, the story of the first Easter is a familiar one: the women going to the tomb early Sunday morning to anoint Jesus' body. Their worry about who would roll away the stone for them. The open tomb. The vacant tomb. The angel announcing Jesus' Resurrection. The women's terror. Their flight. The various appearances of Jesus after the Resurrection—in the upper room, on the seashore, along the road to Emmaus. Yes, it is a familiar story, a beautiful one, and quite incredible.

But the celebration of Easter is more than a wondrous story to be told. It is more than an event that happened to Jesus more than 2,000 years ago. Easter is my story, our story. The Resurrection is in process today in me, in us, here and now. When Jesus rose from the dead, he took all of us with him! He made the power of the Resurrection available to all of us.

Another name for the power of the Resurrection is grace. We can see God's grace being spilled all over the place—if we but take the time to see. I see the power of the Resurrection in places such as these: in a good marriage, in a middle-aged woman caring for her elderly parent, in a young parent tending to a sick child in the middle of the night, in every person of integrity, in a great-grandmother who still has her sense of humor, in the outpouring of help following a natural disaster, in a teacher spending time with a student who needs a little extra help, in a friend who forgives a friend's shortcomings, in someone at prayer, in an ill person who faces death with courage and trust in God.

Pope Benedict XVI has said this about Easter: "Easter is not only a story to be told; it is a signpost on life's way. It is not an account of a miracle that happened a very long time ago; it is a breakthrough which has determined the meaning of all history."

Jesus, may the power of your resurrection fill my life with grace and meaning.

95. *Beginning Anew*

Fragrant Palm Leaves: Journals 1962–1966 is a book by the Buddhist monk and peace activist Thich Nhat Hanh. In the book, Hanh tells of a retreat he once gave for American veterans of the war in Vietnam, his homeland. A number of these veterans were suffering from severe guilt for the things they did or witnessed during the war. One veteran told how almost everyone in his platoon had been killed by guerrillas. In retaliation, the survivors devised a way to kill some of the children in the area. Twenty years later, the image of those children dying haunted this man. Says Hanh: "He was in a living hell."

Hanh shared with the man a Buddhist practice called "beginning anew." He said to him, "You killed five or six children that day? Can you save the lives of five or six children today? Children everywhere in the world are dying because of war, malnutrition, and disease…You still have your body, you still have your heart, you can do many things to help children who are dying in the present moment." The man agreed to do as Hanh suggested, to begin anew.

We all suffer guilt from things we have done, or have not done. Rather than wallowing in guilt for the past, we can use that guilt to transform our actions in the present.

> *Forgiving God, help me to use my guilt for the past to become a more loving person in the present.*

96. *Two Mothers-in-Law in Scripture*

Being a nun, I have never had a mother-in-law. So I have never experienced firsthand the joys and challenges of such a relationship. But I have noticed two mothers-in-law mentioned in Scripture. Both times, the mothers-in-law come out looking good.

The first instance is found in the book of Ruth. Many of us are familiar with the story. Elimelech, wife Naomi, and their two sons emigrate from Judah to Moab due to famine. Their two sons marry Moabite women, Orpah (not Oprah as some of my students thought!) and Ruth. Eventually Elimelech dies along with his two sons.

Naomi decides to return to Judah and tells her two daughters-in-law to remain in Moab, where they will easily find new husbands. But Ruth refuses to stay. She says those words to her mother-in-law that are among the most beautiful in all of Scripture: "Wherever you go I will go, wherever you lodge I will lodge, your people shall be my people, and your God my God" (Ruth 1:16).

Once in Judah, Ruth is discriminated against because she is an outsider. Naomi, however, treats her with nothing but tenderness. (In the 1960 movie version, Naomi is played by Peggy Wood, the perfect choice!) Ruth, for her part, lovingly supports her widowed mother-in-law. The story ends happily. Ruth eventually marries Naomi's "prominent kinsman," Boaz.

The payoff of the story is the genealogy at the end of the book: "Boaz was the father of Obed, Obed was the father of Jesse, and Jesse became the father of David" (Ruth 4:21–22). David, of course, is the great king of Israel. What's more, he is the ancestor of Jesus himself. If Naomi and Ruth had not had such a good relationship, who knows how the story would have ended?

The other mother-in-law belongs to Peter. Her story is told in three short verses. Jesus comes to the home of Peter and Andrew only to find that Peter's mother-in-law is sick "with a fever." Jesus approaches her, grasps her hand, and helps her up. The narrative concludes with: "Then the fever left her and she waited on them" (Mk 1:31).

We know practically nothing about this woman except that she lived with Peter, she was obviously loved by the people who knew her, and she had the inestimable privilege of holding hands with Jesus. What's more, when the fever left her, she immediately began to serve the people gathered in her house—an action we assume was typical for her.

God, be with me in all my relationships—especially those I find challenging.

97. *Humor Can Save Us*

Speaking of mothers-in-law, one woman tells this true story. "My mother-in-law had a wonderful way of telling funny stories that made everyone laugh. After she died, my husband and I moved from New England to North Carolina. One evening we were attending a party with people who didn't know us very well. One person told a funny story that was typical of my mother-in-law's humor. I burst into laughter and said, 'I haven't laughed so hard since Ted's mother died.'"

Laughter is good for the body. Tests have shown it benefits the cardiovascular system as well as the digestive tract. But laughter is also good for the soul. Saint Ignatius wrote, "Laugh and grow strong." He was implying, I believe, that laughter gives us the strength to handle the challenges we meet in life. St. Teresa of Avila prayed, "From sour-faced saints, Good Lord, deliver us!"

Laughter can free us from self-pity. And, as Bernard Basset asks in his book *We Neurotics*, "Is there any human trait less becoming than self-pity, especially when it seeps through to the face?"

Let me conclude this brief reflection on humor with one of my father's favorite stories. I should preface this by saying that my mother often made delicious apple strudel, but sometimes she made it for a party or family gathering.

John was nearing the end of a long life. His children sat around the bed waiting to hear his final words. Finally he said, "Kids, your mother and I have been married for over fifty years. She's a great cook. Even now I can smell the apple strudel she's making in the kitchen. Would one of you please go and get me a piece?"

His daughter left the room. In a few minutes she returned, but without any strudel. "Where's the strudel?" John asked.

She replied, "Mom says you can't have any. It's for the funeral tomorrow."

Source of laughter, deliver me from any self-pity that could stifle my sense of humor.

98. *The Lessons of Life*

Regina Brett, a columnist for Cleveland's *The Plain Dealer*, wrote a column for her forty-fifth birthday a few years back. In it she listed forty-five lessons that life had taught her. When I told her I had used the column for one of the retreats I facilitated, she said, "That column was the most popular column I ever wrote. It generated more mail than anything else I have ever written."

Here are a few of her lessons that I especially liked:

"Life isn't fair, but it's still good."

"It's okay to get angry with God. God can take it."

"Make peace with your past so it doesn't screw up your present."

"You don't have to win every argument. Agree to disagree."

"God loves you because of who God is, not because of anything you did or didn't do."

"No one else is in charge of your happiness. You are the CEO of your joy."

"All that truly matters in the end is that you loved."

"The best is yet to come."

Even if today isn't your birthday, it might be a good day to reflect on the lessons that life has taught you. What, for example, has life taught you about other people, God, love, family, friendship, goodness, suffering, happiness, faith?

> *God of my life, I thank you for all the lessons life is teaching me.*

99. *Small, Imperfect Stones*

Alice Walker's book *Anything We Love Can Be Saved* describes the best-selling author's life of social activism. She tells of her small contributions to the civil rights movement in her early years: She taught in two local black colleges, wrote about the civil rights movement, and produced small history books that were used to teach the teachers of children enrolled in Head Start. But when she measured herself next to some of the giants of social activism—Sojourner Truth, Harriet Tubman, Mahatma Gandhi, Martin Luther King Jr.—she felt very inferior. She writes, "[My] small stone of activism [did] not seem to measure up to the rugged boulders of heroism [I] so admired."

Walker also says that many people believe their contributions to any movement are too small, too insignificant, too inferior to count. Hence, "they choose to withhold their offerings out of shame." Walker calls such a withholding "the tragedy of the world." She goes on to assert her conviction that if we want to change the world for the better, we must bring "our small, imperfect stones to the pile."

What wise words! The old proverb says, "The perfect is often the enemy of the good." None of us is perfect. We all have flaws. Even our greatest heroes have flaws. But the awareness of our imperfection must never deter us from making a contribution to the betterment of our world. Walker goes on to say, "But it is the awareness of having faults, I think, and the knowledge that this links us to everyone on earth, that opens us to courage and compassion."

God of my deepest convictions, help me to bring my small, imperfect stone to the pile.

100. *Freedom: Doing What I Ought*

What is freedom? Some think it is the state of having permanent options. "I don't want to make any commitments, because I want to be free." But this view of freedom falls short, for the only benefit of having options is to eventually choose something. Others might say that freedom is doing whatever we want to do. But a person who makes destructive choices—for example, to use drugs—is certainly not free.

I like what Pope John Paul II said about freedom: "Freedom consists not in doing what you like, but in having the right to do what you ought." The word "ought" implies that some choices are better than others. They go beyond merely doing what I would like to do. Aung San Suu Kyi, who was awarded the Nobel Peace Prize for her work for democracy in Myanmar (Burma), said this about freedom: "To be free is to be able to do what you think is right...It is a united determination to persevere in the struggle, to make sacrifices in the name of enduring truths."

What inhibits us from being truly free? Sometimes outside forces do. Aung San Suu Kyi, for example, has spent many years in prison and under house arrest because of her activism. In one sense, then, she is not free. But on a deeper level, she is freer than even her persecutors, for she is willing to make incredible sacrifices in the name of the enduring truth called democracy. She once said, "The only real prison is fear, and the only real freedom is freedom from fear."

Often the price we pay for freedom is uncertainty. Sadly, some people, because of fear, choose certainty over liberation, security over emancipation. How free am I? What holds me back from being truly free?

Liberating God, help me to persevere in the struggle for the freedom to do what I ought.

INDEX

The numbers indicate the number of the reflection

addiction, 37, 100

adversity, 8, 11, 33, 36, 42, 49, 53, 67, 68, 70, 73, 91, 93

aging, 2, 15, 22, 46, 49, 54, 62, 66, 67, 69, 75, 91

animals, 9, 10, 26, 32, 38, 45, 53

Annunciation, 82

apples, 28

art, 71

attention (awareness), 6, 14, 25, 35, 38, 39, 48, 51, 63, 80, 86, 98

beauty, 6, 25, 40, 71, 91

Catherine of Siena, 8

change, 22, 26, 43, 93

children, 16, 24, 34, 90

Christmas, 52, 64

community, 30

compassion (*see also* love), 12, 23, 58, 67, 99

consumerism, 52

courage, 2, 8, 36, 70, 74, 84, 88, 99

dance, 77

darkness, 8, 12, 21, 49, 61, 67, 72, 95

death, 9, 47, 66, 75, 79

detachment, 56, 75

discipleship, 1, 5, 12, 18, 27, 57, 60, 68

dispossession, 56

doubt, 21, 84

Easter, 94

evil, 4, 8, 25, 67

faith, 8, 11, 21, 27, 38, 40, 43, 60, 88

family, 16, 54, 96

flight, 9

forgiveness, 1, 3, 87, 95

freedom, 37, 100

friendship, 18, 83

funerals, 75

future, 47, 69, 89

God, 6, 7, 20, 42, 44, 48, 65,
    80, 81, 87, 88, 90

goodness, 3, 25, 84, 89, 99

gratitude, 28, 41, 63

grief, 36, 67, 75

growth, 22

guilt, 3, 95

healing, 43

heaven, 9, 67

hope, 4, 27, 65, 89

humor, 2, 16, 46, 62, 97

Incarnation, 90

imperfections, 62, 65, 95, 99

jealousy, 2, 24

Jesus, 5, 18, 27, 35, 52, 60, 61,
    77, 86, 90

Joseph, 68

justice, 3, 12, 30, 39, 58, 74,
    89, 99

leadership, 13, 19

letting go, 56, 75

life, 8, 25, 53, 63, 69, 78, 98

love, 1, 12, 23, 61, 64, 67, 85,
    87, 92, 96

Mary, 33, 82

mercy, 1, 87

miracles, 43, 63

mourning (see grief)

music, 15, 36

mystery, 4, 25, 28, 32, 40, 63,
    88, 91

nature, 6, 9, 24, 26, 28, 31, 32,
    38, 40, 43, 45, 53, 63, 91

patience, 43, 65, 70, 73

Paul, 57

pausing, 78

perspective, 6, 8, 25, 34, 46,
    69, 81, 90

prayer, 10, 14, 17, 31, 80

prophets, 3, 74

puzzles, 73

quotations, 19, 44, 70, 76

Resurrection, 76, 94

saints, 29

Scripture (Bible), 15, 35, 37,
    55, 66, 82, 87, 93, 94, 96

security, 27, 37, 88

seeking, 20, 55

self-esteem, 51, 60

service, 23, 55

sickness, 43, 50

sin, 3, 55, 60, 67, 95

sleep, 7

spring, 76

suffering (pain), 8, 25, 43, 47, 50, 56, 67, 85, 95

survival, 53

thanksgiving (*see* gratitude)

trust, 11, 42, 48, 61, 70, 88

walking, 31

watching, 49

waiting, 43, 49, 86

winter, 72

wonder, 22, 28, 32, 38, 40, 43, 63

work, 29

writing, 17

zeal, 57

ALSO BY
SR. MELANNIE SVOBODA

Just Because *Prayer-Poems to Delight the Heart*

These prayer-poems have the uncanny ability to put readers in the presence of the universal and eternal, thus connecting them with God, others, with nature, and the entire world.

128 pages ◆ **$12.95** ◆ **order 957743** ◆ **978-1-58595-774-3**

With the Dawn Rejoicing *A Christian Perspective on Pain and Suffering*

This deeply spiritual exploration of pain offers encouragement for anyone dealing with suffering—whether physical, psychological, or spiritual. It is rooted in Scripture and real life and touches on the many ways pain affects our lives.

144 pages ◆ **$12.95** ◆ **order 956999** ◆ **978-1-58595-699-9**

When the Rain Speaks *Celebrating God's Presence in Nature*

Sr. Melannie has a gift for describing everyday experiences of nature as mystical adventures. This is a wonderful spirituality book for adults of all ages and a gift book that will be cherished.

160 pages ◆ **$12.95** ◆ **order 956845** ◆ **978-1-58595-684-5**

In Steadfast Love *Letters on the Spiritual Life*

One of the best spiritual writers of our day offers this wonderful collection of letters on the spiritual life. She believes that no matter what one's call might be, we are all dealing with similar challenges.

168 pages ◆ **$14.95** ◆ **order 956289** ◆ **978-1-58595-628-9**

When the Moon Slips Away *Rejoicing in Everyday Miracles*

Each of these beautiful meditations begins with a thought-provoking quotation, has questions for personal reflection and/or communal sharing, and offers a short prayer that flows from the reflection.

144 pages ◆ **$12.95** ◆ **order 957286** ◆ **978-1-58595-728-6**

1-800-321-0411
www.23rdpublications.com

TWENTY
THIRD
PUBLICATIONS